ESTER

ADDICTED TO FOOTBALL

ADDICTED TO FOOTBALL

MY JOURNEY FROM ANFIELD TO ALMOST EVERYWHERE

JON NEWBY

pitch

First published by Pitch Publishing, 2022

Pitch Publishing
A2 Yeoman Gate
Yeoman Way
Worthing
Sussex
BN13 3QZ
www.pitchpublishing.co.uk
info@pitchpublishing.co.uk

A CIP catalogue record is available for this book
from the British Library.

ISBN 978 1 80150 073 9

Typesetting and origination by Pitch Publishing

Printed and bound in India by Replika Press Pvt. Ltd.

Contents

TO MY FAMILY

For my mum and dad, who gave me the love and opportunity to succeed with everything that they did for me. You were and still are always there for me.

For my brother David, who for years travelled all over the country to watch me. Your support always meant more than you will ever know and kept me going on the bad days.

For my amazing wife Wendy, who had to put up with all my moods after the bad games. You were the one who always believed in me and never stopped supporting me, both on and most importantly off the pitch. That meant everything to me.

For my children Josh and Olivia, my best friends, who make me proud every day. Watching you both score goals now makes me happier than if I'd scored again myself.

I love you all.

Foreword by Hugh McAuley

JON WAS nine years old when I first spotted him playing for Formby Junior Sports Club alongside my son Barry.

Jon's dad Jim and I would be at the boys' game early on a Sunday afternoon to help set up the goals, along with the other parents whose lads played in the local Craven Minor Junior Football League.

At that young age Jon would always show the confidence in his natural ability and self-belief to run past opposing players with and without the ball. Throughout that first season he would use his exceptional speed to score many individual goals; he was always desperate to score, and thrived on any passes or crosses that came his way in and around the penalty area.

As a natural footballer these were the traits that always stood out in his game, scoring regularly and taking the eye against any team Formby played. It was an excellent little side with a lot of the youngsters ending up playing at a really good level.

Little did Jon know that those early development days would eventually lead to him playing on the hallowed turf of Anfield for Liverpool Football Club at first-team level.

It was at this time that Dave Shannon and I were asked by Liverpool to help set up a new centre of excellence and, soon after, the club appointed Steve Heighway as the new youth development officer. These were exciting times and Jon was one of a fantastic group of young, aspiring footballers invited to the newly formed youth system, which also included Robbie Fowler, Dominic Matteo, Phil Charnock, David Thompson, Steven Gerrard and Michael Owen.

At that time Kenny Dalglish was the first-team manager and he was keen for us to develop local players. He would often come along to the sessions at the Vernon Sangster sports centre opposite Anfield to support his son Paul and would inevitably end up playing in the five-a-side game with the boys, which always finished the session off.

Following his expected development, Jon progressed to full-time training and made his mark at youth-team level when we won the FA Youth Cup for the first time in the club's history in 1996.

Jon made his first-team debut in the League Cup against Hull City in 1999 and we were all extremely pleased for him. He left two years later to join Bury to further his career and play regular first-team football.

It was always a pleasure to work with Newbs in those formative years and to this day we are still very good friends and speak regularly. He now uses all his experience working full time in the recruitment department at Liverpool's academy, identifying talented young players hoping to follow the same path and live their dream of wearing the red shirt of Liverpool Football Club at Anfield.

Jon was a model professional. He was a credit to himself, his family and his profession.

Hughie McAuley

Introduction

IT WAS a freezing February afternoon in Darwen near Blackburn. The rain, which had been coming down almost sideways, had turned into hailstones that were literally bouncing off the astroturf pitch.

I could hardly see my team-mates, let alone the ball, as the weather got worse. My hands were absolutely freezing and apart from the managers and subs of both teams there was nobody watching; nobody at all, not even one man and his dog.

Why? Well not many people ever watched the Manchester Amateur League Bridgewater Cup semi-final at the best of times, let alone in this weather – or so I'm led to believe. It was the first time I had played in this competition.

Yet a minute later I controlled a pass with my right foot and smashed it past the Springhead goalkeeper with my left from just inside the box to bring us level at 1-1 and I forgot about the cold, I forgot about how sore my Achilles was feeling on the hard surface of the pitch and instead felt one of the best feelings in the world, scoring a goal.

In that split second I could have been back at Anfield playing for Liverpool. It didn't matter that I was only playing for the Walshaw Sports A team, or the Walshaw Legends as we preferred to be called. It was a goal and I would never get tired of scoring goals no matter who I was playing for.

This is the story about my life as a lower-league footballer who simply couldn't give the game up. Most of the time I have loved football, on occasions I have hated it, but for years it has taken over my life.

It is a story that gives an insight in to what it is like trying to make a living in the unpredictable world of lower-league football. It starts as a young boy dreaming of playing for Liverpool and takes twists and turns through eight tiers of English football.

On the way there is elation, despair, and serious injury along with a spell in management, battles with my own mind and, as my career ended, a condition so serious that heart surgery was the only option.

Prologue

YOU SEE defibrillators used in television dramas. This wasn't television. This was real life. My life.

The surgeon counted down from five to zero. I had no idea what was coming.

Boom!

The shock hit me like nothing I had ever experienced in my life as the electrical current went through me and I felt my body jump off the operating table.

Most people have defibrillators used on them when they are unconscious, but I was wide awake. The power and force of the shock was unbelievable.

A few years earlier, on 8 March 2014, I hadn't long been playing for Walshaw when I collapsed on the pitch following a 30-yard sprint against Elton. An ambulance was called and I spent the rest of the day in hospital wired up to all kinds of machines but was discharged later that night after nothing untoward was found in any of my tests.

Over the next few years, I would regularly have dizzy spells when playing. The managers at Walshaw even began to fill their pockets with glucose energy sweets at games and would throw them on to the pitch to me hoping it would help if I didn't feel right, but no doctors could get to the bottom of the situation.

I was often rushing to games as I was at work on a Saturday morning and probably wasn't eating as well as I should have been ahead of a match. The doctors even felt it could be something as simple as low blood sugar levels or dehydration.

As things got worse and I suffered two more collapses over the next few months, once while coaching and another while playing, I saw a doctor called Nick Jenkins who was painstaking in his quest to find out what was wrong. He saw enough to send me to London to St George's Hospital in London to see Professor Sanjay Sharma, who specialised in athletes with cardiac conditions. I went through various ECG and exercise tests on treadmills and bikes before I went into his office to speak to him.

I already knew that something wasn't right. You don't keep collapsing for no reason, but I wasn't expecting the news to be quite so bad.

He showed me my ECG readings from my exercise tests. There were no regular up-and-down lines of a heartbeat on one of the pages. Instead, it was like a kid had scribbled all over the page.

'This is a major concern. I don't like the look of it at all,' Professor Sharma told me. He said that although my heart was strong, the electrical part of it simply didn't work properly. My heart rate had touched 230bpm on the bike out of nowhere, and, had I not been as fit as I was, one of my previous collapses would have killed me. If I continued to exercise as much as I was then I was at very high risk of sudden cardiac death.

The words 'you shouldn't be here' aren't easy to digest. It wasn't something you expect to hear. My first thoughts after it weren't about the fact my life was in danger and what was to happen next. Even though it was now 2018 and I hadn't played competitively for nearly two years, one of my first questions to the surgeon was, 'Can I still play football?'

It was bizarre how as a sportsman my mind worked. This was a life-and-death situation and all I could think about was joining in the five-a-sides with the lads first thing on a Tuesday morning before we started work for the day at Liverpool's academy.

His answer was emphatic, 'No.'

'Medication, no exercise over 100bpm and we will try and control it,' was his message over and over again. It would be beyond difficult for me to adjust my life from someone who had trained at such a high intensity for the last 20 years to now doing nothing more than a walk.

On 21 March 2019 I travelled back to London with my wife Wendy for a heart surgery procedure called an ablation. During the operation, tubes are pushed through your groins and travel up to your heart through blood vessels. The surgeons then attempt to burn the faulty pathways in your heart. It isn't a pleasant operation, and can last for up to six hours. You are awake throughout the surgery and your heart is stimulated so it can be set to different speeds to find out exactly where the abnormal rhythms are coming from.

At the beginning of the surgery my heart rate dropped to 17bpm and it was the worst I had ever felt in my life. I genuinely felt like I was dying, just fading away, and I remember frantically looking around the operating theatre for someone to help me even though the surgeons had everything under control.

Three hours into the operation with my heart beating at just over 200bpm, I noticed a bit of 'excitement' in the room with the surgeon calling a few other doctors in and saying he had found what he was looking for inside my heart. I also heard him tell the nurses to prepare to shock. They weren't able to bring my heart rate back down to a normal rhythm and it just kept rising. Unless they shocked me with a defibrillator I was likely to go into cardiac arrest.

The noise the machine made as it shocked me will stay in my mind forever. If I close my eyes, I can be back on that operating table hearing that sound. However, it had helped to save my life.

The operation was stopped straight away and as the surgeon stood over me, he said very matter-of-factly, 'You've got ARVC.'

Arrhythmogenic right ventricular cardiomyopathy was the one condition we had spoken about in the lead-up to the operation that we hoped it wouldn't be. It was the absolute worst-case scenario for me and at that moment I knew my life had changed forever.

1

I want to play for Liverpool

I WAS the same as any other young kid. I dreamt of playing for the team I supported, and that team was Liverpool.

My bedroom was completely covered in Liverpool posters, Dalglish and Rush especially, and as I got a bit older, John Barnes. I remember the first time I stood on the Kop in the late 1980s to watch a 0-0 draw against West Ham, I was disappointed I hadn't been able to celebrate a goal but I couldn't wait to go back.

Until then I had always sat in the Anfield Road End or The Paddock, but there was something special about the Kop. Queuing outside to pay your £4 to get in, the stairs up to the terrace, seeing the green of the pitch come into view and then finding your spec to watch the game. And then the noise, the songs, the flags, the colours, the atmosphere. There was no place like it.

I would be fortunate in that I would go on to play 70 minutes in front of the Kop for Liverpool, although those first-team appearances at Anfield seem a lifetime ago.

My first football team was Penketh United in Warrington, where we lived until I was nine. We lived in the Great Sankey area of the town – me, my mum and dad, and my older brother David.

My parents were hard-working people. My mum, originally from Leicester, was a teacher and my dad, who was from Old Swan in Liverpool, worked at the Ford car plant in Halewood.

I used to love chasing his car up the road when he was working nights, seeing if I could beat him to the end of our street to show him how fast I was.

As a kid all I did was play football. If I wasn't playing or training for my Saturday team, I would be on the street usually with David and his mates outside our house using the green gates as the goal.

If there was nobody to play with it didn't bother me. I would be doing kick-ups or shooting by myself.

One of my earliest football memories is from 1986 on the day Liverpool were away at Chelsea and a win would clinch the league title. I was on my own playing football in the street and one of my neighbours walked past and told me Kenny Dalglish had just given us the lead.

I remember smashing the ball high in the air celebrating and running inside to check the score on *Grandstand* and then coming back out and trying to recreate the type of goal I thought Dalglish had just scored.

I played up front and all I wanted to do was score goals. Nothing felt as good as the ball hitting the back of the net. I played on Saturday and Sunday mornings and occasionally Sunday afternoon too. If there was only one game for me on the Sunday, my dad would take me to the field and pass the ball to my left foot constantly trying to improve that.

There was no getting bored on computers or the Xbox in your bedroom. In the summer we would play cricket outside the house or go on bike rides, but other than that it was just football, football and more football.

We moved from Warrington to Formby in March 1988, the weekend Everton ended Liverpool's 29-game unbeaten start to that particular season, and that year was when I first went to Liverpool's Centre of Excellence as a nine-year-old.

One of the coaches there at the time was Hugh McAuley, and he was watching his son Barry play for Formby Juniors Sports

Club, the local team I had just joined on moving to the area. After impressing Hughie I began to train once a week at Litherland High School. There were no state-of-the-art academy facilities in those days, just an hour a week in a sports hall with a few footballs. That was it.

The coaches when I started at Liverpool were Hughie, Dave Shannon and legendary Liverpool winger Steve Heighway.

I stayed at Liverpool until I was 22 so I never knew any other youth coaches and I may be biased, but to me H, Dave and Steve are without doubt up there with the best youth football coaches this country has ever seen. They brought through McManaman, Fowler, Matteo, Carragher, Thompson, Gerrard and Owen. How much would that lot cost in today's market?

Even back then they wanted to make you a better person as well as a better player. They had standards that they had learnt as players with Steve and H both having been at Liverpool for a long time.

All three of the coaches demanded focus and concentration in every training session and when I see them work these days, they are exactly the same. About five years ago Steve was taking a session with the under-14s and asked a few of the coaches – me, Mike Yates and Phil Charnock – to join in. We had all been at the club as boys so knew how Steve worked, but even on that day we all said afterwards that when he said well done to one of us during the session, we got the same buzz out of it as if we were 12 again. He was still the man we wanted to impress, even at 37! That's how important he was to all of us as players.

Liverpool as a football club still has those same standards now. You couldn't fail to become both a better person and a better player when training with the coaches. Even at such a young age you didn't want to be the one who made a mistake and give that Adidas tango away. It was a healthy fear, though, and at no stage was anyone afraid to express themselves on the ball.

The message back then was all about passing the ball. Pass and move, and if you needed to dribble make sure you had something in your locker to get out of trouble.

I can still hear Dave Shannon shouting, 'It's like watching Boca Juniors!' when one of us played a one-two. It was the best footballing education that I could wish for growing up and was kept so simple.

As the years progressed at Liverpool, I just kept getting asked to come back. I enjoyed it so I kept going and every now and then we would get a night where we would train at Anfield and imagine we were playing for the first-team.

Often we would train on the all-weather pitch at Melwood, but back then that all-weather pitch was shale. There was no artificial turf, just gravel that had puddles all over it when it rained and scraped your legs to bits if you fell over, but if it was good enough for Barnes, Beardsley and Rush then it was good enough for us.

When we trained on the grass pitches at Melwood we would normally just play a match among ourselves and you were hoping to be on the team that got to wear the red shirts with Candy on the front and a number on the back. 'Number ten, I got Barnes!' you'd hear from the crowd of excited kids. It was a massive thrill just to pull the shirt on at the place where our heroes trained.

I remember signing schoolboy forms for Liverpool on 29 January 1993 and being very proud, but I didn't see it as a big deal – I just loved playing football.

I was 14 then, but still tiny and as skinny as a rake, and Dave Shannon had given me the nickname Bambi as apparently I had legs thinner than the deer in the film. It is the name Dave still calls me now every time I see him at Liverpool.

Those skinny legs could run, though. I was lightning quick, scored a lot of goals and had a footballing brain – and with the help of Hughie, Steve and Dave I kept progressing.

I had a year during the under-15 age group where I struggled. I was growing and that seemed to hinder my pace, which in turn affected my confidence. I was very quiet as a kid in the Liverpool environment and when I wasn't playing well my confidence would be affected further, which would be something I would struggle with throughout my career.

It was at under-16 level when things started to become a bit more serious, because that was the season where you would be offered YTS forms at the club or be released.

I was fortunate that this would be one of my best seasons. I can even remember the game when everything seemed to click. We played Blackburn at Melwood on the B-team pitch one Sunday morning in November.

Before then I had been progressing steadily, but that morning things seemed to fall into place and I didn't look back. I scored one in a 3-0 win and followed it up by putting one in the top corner the week later at Littleton Road in Salford as we beat Manchester United 4-2. I then scored two against Everton a week or so after that.

Even back then there was no better feeling than scoring against Everton. In recent times Liverpudlians have seen Manchester United as our main rivals, but for me it's always been Everton and always will be.

Even now I hate derby day. Even with a watching brief. I can't eat on the day of the derby because I'm that nervous.

That day as a 16-year-old, both of my goals in the 3-0 win were set up by Steven Gerrard. As a forward you were delighted if you knew Stevie was playing in midfield behind you because if you made a run, he would find you. His vision and range of passing even then was outstanding and nobody doubted he would go on and be the player he was for Liverpool.

Back then there were a lot of local lads at the club. As well as Steven there was Tommy Culshaw, a no-nonsense centre-half who is now a first-team coach at Glasgow Rangers, Stephen Wright, who played for Liverpool's first-team, Michael Yates who has been at the club for over 25 years as player and now coach, and

Andy Parkinson who had a successful league career, plus many others like them.

All of these players had been at Liverpool from a very early age, like me, and lived in or around the city. We knew how lucky we were to represent the club and the standards were drummed into us by the staff very early in our time there.

Steve, H and Dave were our coaches and mentors and letting them down was not an option. As players we all came through the ranks together and we knew we were in a position that many other boys in the city were desperate to be in playing for a club like Liverpool.

We travelled abroad for European competitions, and I can remember playing Barcelona in one final at under-16 level in France and us being nervous standing alongside the Spanish team in the tunnel waiting to go out on to the pitch. Our physio Frank Skelly started to sing 'You'll Never Walk Alone'. We all joined in and belted out the anthem together, stood in the cramped stone tunnel, and the words echoed which made it sound even louder. Even now the hairs on my neck stand up when I think about it.

Barcelona didn't know what to make of it standing there right next to a group of lads belting this famous anthem out and, coincidence or not, we scored in the first 25 seconds. That was our way of saying, 'We are Liverpool.'

The end of that under-16 season was always going to be interesting. I had been offered YTS forms but I was never going to be able to sign them. My mum was big on my education, being a teacher, and there was no way she was going to let me leave school without doing my A levels and having something to fall back on as she put it, should the football not work out – and there was no guarantee it would.

Of all the boys who join a club aged nine, like I did, only an extremely low percentage go on and play for the first-team or have a lasting career in the game at all.

My dad, on the other hand, would have loved me to sign for Liverpool there and then. He had grown up in the city with my nan and grandad and his four brothers. The whole family were massive Liverpool supporters and had been going to the match for years.

To see a Newby play for Liverpool was a dream for them. I'm sure there were many arguments between my parents as to whether I was going to be allowed to sign these YTS forms, but in the end my mum won and officially becoming a Liverpool player would have to wait for a year or so.

I think in the long term staying at school may have done me a favour. Some of the lads found it hard being at Melwood from 8.30am until 4.30pm every day and I don't know whether being quiet would have seen me swallowed up in that environment, coming straight out of school.

My schedule was very different from the rest of the lads. I continued training two nights a week as I had done for the previous few seasons, but with the age group below me, and then I would play in the A or B team on a Saturday. I felt fresh and looked forward to my football at the weekend after a week at school and I was full of energy and confidence.

That season was my first experience of the FA Youth Cup, the major competition in youth football throughout the whole country. As I was still at school I didn't expect to be involved and in the first two rounds I wasn't, but the regular forwards Michael Johnson and David Larmour were both injured for the next round and I had been playing very well in the B team so I found myself selected for the game against Sheffield United at Anfield.

The other forward selected alongside me didn't train at the club every day either. He was based at the FA National School at Lilleshall and if I thought I was quick then my strike partner was like Road Runner and he could put the ball in the back of the net better than anyone I've ever seen. His name? Michael Owen.

In those days all the clubs used to play their FA Youth Cup games at the first-team ground rather than being pushed out to a local non-league or rugby ground, and I remember sitting in the dressing room at Anfield before the game being unbelievably nervous.

The stadium seemed massive during the warm-up and every shout could be heard with not many people in the crowd. The game itself was physically very tough – they kicked us all over the place – but I scored my first goal at Anfield when Stuart Quinn crossed from the right and I slid in to finish with my left foot at the Anfield Road End as we won 3-2, with Michael scoring the other two goals.

We were into the quarter-final where we drew Manchester United, again at home. It was a much tougher game and I remember finding it hard against the centre-half pairing of John Curtis and Ronnie Wallwork, both of whom would go on to have long careers in the top divisions. We went 2-0 down with only 15 minutes or so left, just enough time for Michael to score three quick goals at the Kop end for a 3-2 win.

It wouldn't be the last hat-trick he would score for Liverpool and we all knew that then. He was without doubt the most single-minded footballer I ever played with. His self-belief was unbelievable. Nothing fazed him, he played with no fear at all and lived to score goals, and, had he not suffered with the horrendous hamstring tear at Elland Road when he was still young, I believe he would have gone on to be England's record goalscorer.

The semi-final saw us paired against Crystal Palace with the first leg being at Anfield. We won 4-2 with another hat-trick from Michael, and travelled to London for the away leg a couple of weeks later, staying at a hotel in Croydon the night before the game.

I remember the coaches being very nervous in the build-up. The club had never won the FA Youth Cup and there was a real buzz about this team with a lot of people in the city talking about Owen, Jamie Carragher and David Thompson in particular.

I hit the bar twice in the first 20 minutes of the game, once with either foot. I hoped it wasn't going to be one of those nights. Half an hour later it looked like it was as we found ourselves 3-0 down and trailing 5-4 on aggregate. Palace had two very strong, quick forwards in Clinton Morrison and Leon McKenzie, and they were causing our defence no end of problems.

Jamie Cassidy, our left-winger, brought us level in the tie with 20 minutes to go and the result was back in the balance. I was substituted soon after wards but I couldn't really complain. I hadn't played poorly, but it showed the fine line between success and failure as a striker.

If both my finishes had been an inch lower in the first half then I'd have been the hero, but that was a striker's life and something I would get to understand well over the next 15 years.

The game went into extra time and Michael bagged another two as we drew 3-3 to send us through to a two-legged final against a very talented West Ham United team.

The first leg was at Upton Park and we were without Michael, as he was playing for England in an international tournament, so I was partnered up front by Andy Parkinson.

All the talk before the game was about a centre-half coming through at West Ham who was already being spoken of as a future England player, a certain Rio Ferdinand. They also had Frank Lampard in midfield, so it showed the quality that was on show in the final that year.

We had a team full of personality and characters, Scouse lads who could play, but when needed could battle as well. Roy Naylor was our keeper. Lee Prior was our right-back and up there as one of the funniest characters I ever met in the game, and someone I would have hated to play against, while Phil Brazier and Jamie Carragher were in the middle of the back four and Welshman Gareth Roberts was at left-back.

Two talented Scousers played wide in midfield, Stuart Quinn on the right and Jamie Cassidy on the left, with David Thompson and Mark Quinn in the centre of the park and me and Andy Parkinson up front. Most of us had been at the club since we were about ten years old, and this was the biggest game we had played in with about 20,000 people packed into Upton Park.

I think Steve, H and Dave were more nervous than us in the build-up and a memory that sticks in my mind is the team coach pulling up outside at a pub on the way to the match and the three of them heading inside for five minutes – clearly for a quick drink to settle the nerves!

When we returned to the dressing room after our warm-up, we were boosted by seeing first-team manager Roy Evans and his assistant Doug Livermore, as they had a game in London the following night. There was no big speech from either of them; that wasn't the Liverpool style. It was just a quick 'good luck and enjoy it' before they left us to it.

H gave us his usual team talk about working hard first and foremost. 'Win your battle and then you can play,' he would say. To this day I know his chat before a game would be very similar no matter what team he was coaching. Tactically H was very clever, and we would work on tactics during the week in training, but before a game it would be about working hard and earning the right to play.

I can't remember too much about the match itself, other than the two chances I had in the first 25 minutes. The first was after Stuey Quinn skipped past his full-back on the right and pulled it back to me near the penalty spot and I used the pace on the ball to side-foot it high into the roof of the net as Rio Ferdinand closed me down. I peeled away to my left, my heart nearly leaping out of my chest and was mobbed by the rest of the lads.

The game was live on Sky Sports, so it wasn't a bad time to score. My second chance came a few minutes later from Cass down the left who pulled it back. I caught it perfectly with my left foot, but this time the keeper made a magnificent save, tipping it around the post to keep the score 1-0 going into the break.

As I was not training full time, I wasn't at the same fitness level as the other lads and was replaced after about 70 minutes, with David Larmour coming on to grab a second goal. We were heading back to Anfield with a 2-0 lead.

I didn't sleep a wink that night when I got home, but there was no rest for me the following day as I'd already had two days off school for the match. There was no warm-down and massage at Melwood, just double history at school!

There were about ten days before the return leg but it was hard to focus on anything else. The game was all that mattered to us. We were 2-0 up, we had Michael Owen returning and would have an expected 25,000 crowd behind us at Anfield. Nothing could go wrong, could it?

It did, after just 47 seconds, when the ball fell to Frank Lampard on the edge of the box and he smashed it high into the Kop goal. West Ham were right-back in the game and with Rio Ferdinand playing further forward they were looking a real threat.

Our nerves were calmed when Michael bundled home an equaliser minutes before half-time and when Stuey Quinn smashed a left-footed drive home at the Kop end midway through the second half, we knew the cup was ours for the first time in the club's history.

It was an amazing feeling walking round Anfield celebrating in a front of a packed Kop end and like all the boys that night I hoped I would be doing similar in a first-team shirt in years to come, although none of us were under any illusions of how difficult it was going to be to break into that first XI.

Those FA Youth Cup days were special. Even the players who went on and played at the very top will still look back on that year as being memorable. The characters in that dressing room were some of the best lads I would meet in my career and the togetherness, whether you were a massive personality or one of the quieter lads like me, was unbelievable.

The cup that year was won mainly by mentality. We were never beaten even if it seemed like there was no way back. No egos, just Merseyside lads who were willing to give absolutely everything for each other and realised just how much it meant to play for Liverpool.

Some of the stories from inside that dressing room could fill a book on their own but many couldn't be printed! Football dressing rooms are very different places these days, and maybe that's for the best, but that Melwood dressing room was character-building and no place for lads who couldn't play.

One story that still makes me laugh involves a lad who had been told he wasn't getting a contract at the end of his YTS days and although he still trained at Liverpool during the week, he would go on trial at other clubs at the weekend from about April onwards hoping to find a new club.

At the time Stan Collymore was at Liverpool and was one of the first players to wear coloured boots, with his choice being a distinctive bright red Diadora pair.

One Friday these red boots went missing from the boot room at Melwood and that afternoon we had first Ronnie Moran, then Sammy Lee and finally H reading the riot act to us with the younger lads under firm suspicion as culprits as to where they had vanished to. By the end of the day the boots still hadn't turned up and reluctantly the staff let us all go home.

The following day most of us were playing for the A team and when we turned up to the away game that Saturday morning, the lad who was in the process of being released was in the opposition dressing room playing against us as a trialist.

You can imagine the scenes as he jogged out for the warm-up with a big grin on his face pointing down at the red Diadora boots on his feet. He even commented on the comfort of his newly acquired footwear as he ambled past us. Even H had to laugh and with the boots back on Collymore's peg first thing on Monday morning not a word was said to the first-team staff.

They were funny days with some unbelievable characters. The season after the FA Youth Cup win, 1996/97, was also my last year at school. I would finish my exams in the summer of '97 and sign my first professional contract. It was also the first time that my confidence would really affect my performances.

I was someone who analysed my own performances far too much for someone so young. Running through the game in your mind afterwards is normal for any footballer but I just couldn't switch off. I also doubted myself massively and this would hinder me a great deal over my career.

I was a massive confidence player. If I was playing or scoring, I felt like I could do anything on the pitch, even against top players, but if I was struggling with my confidence I could go the other way and look like I'd never kicked a ball before in my life. Mentally I wasn't strong enough and that is a quality that separates the good players from the great.

I remember speaking to H about it. 'You're three weeks away from signing a professional contract at Liverpool Football Club. That should give you all the confidence you need,' he said. He was right, of course, but doubting myself on the pitch would go on for most of my career.

Two weeks later I did as H had said and became a professional at Liverpool. It was a very proud moment not just for me but for my family as well. My dad and my brother David were big Liverpool fans and I had been going all over the country with David following the Reds on the infamous Barnes Travel coaches for years – and it felt great making that transition from fan to player.

My first contract was a far cry from what most first year professionals earn these days. In the summer of 1997, the deal I signed for £250 a week with a signing-on fee of £2,600 wasn't going to make me rich, but I had a chance to do what millions of people throughout the world could only dream of.

I found that first year as a pro extremely hard. The change and the step up from being at school to training with the likes of Robbie Fowler, Steve McManaman and Jamie Redknapp every day was massive and I can honestly say it took me the best part of the entire season to adjust.

Pre-season was a real eye-opener at that level. All the young professionals joined the first-team players, and the fitness levels were unbelievable. McManaman and Jason McAteer could run all day; Dom Matteo was another. It seemed effortless to them. I was a sprinter so the longer running was a killer for me, especially with Ronnie Moran and Sammy Lee shouting 'encouragement' at us and no doubt seeing what character the young lads had.

One run in particular was a nightmare, the 8-80s. It took up all three pitches at Melwood and was the one that everyone dreaded. You would arrive at the training ground and see the poles set up and your heart would sink. Neil Ruddock would be close to tears when the shout went up to head out to the pitches on 8-80s day. I wasn't far behind him!

I was still living with my mum and dad at the time in Formby and used to drive in with a couple of other lads living nearby, Paul Dalglish and Ian Dunbavin. They were two real characters, especially Bavo. He was a keeper, and they are always a bit different, but Bavo was and still is crazy.

There were many times I'd pick him up and he'd come running out of his house and jump in the car with his bowl of cereal still in his hand. Five minutes later the window would go down and he would throw his bowl and spoon out of the window on the Formby bypass. He did it most days for a couple of weeks and after that never again, presumably because he had run out of anything to eat his cereal from! He was a good keeper and went on to have a long league career with the likes of Accrington Stanley and Chesterfield.

The season itself was tough. I mainly played for the A team and got my fair share of goals, but on the few occasions I played in the reserves I found it hard playing against experienced professionals. One game at Preston North End sticks in the mind in which we had an experienced line up with Tony Warner, Razor Ruddock, Steve Harkness and Stig Inge Bjørnebye playing, and we got beat 3-0. I hardly got a kick and was dragged off after an hour. Welcome to the real world!

I got my next chance to start for the 'ressies' a few weeks later against Tranmere Rovers, a game played at Chester's Deva stadium, and I got my first goal at that level firing in after Steven Gerrard whipped a low cross in to the box.

I started the remaining reserve team games that season including a 1-0 win against Manchester United at Bury's Gigg Lane where I played on the right wing in what was probably my best game of the season. It drew praise from Ronnie Moran, which even first-team players would tell you is rare, but three days later after a game at Stoke City's Britannia Stadium he brought me back down to earth with a bollocking that far outweighed the positive comments earlier in the week.

That was just his way and he would never let anyone get carried away with performances, whether they were a first-team player or a youngster. They could always do better. He kept everyone grounded in true Liverpool style and that is what made him such a legend throughout all his years at the club.

My contract was up at the end of the season, though, and deep down I didn't think I had done enough to be offered another one so I was preparing myself for the worst.

Roy Evans was the manager and ultimately the decision was his. As young professionals we trained separately from the first-team squad with coach Sammy Lee, and the manager would be guided by him. My only problem was that I didn't think Sammy was having me as a player either.

I knew Roy was going to be speaking to a few of us after training one particular day, and I happened to bump into Steve Heighway along the corridor at Melwood half an hour before

I was due to see the manager. I mentioned to Steve that it was decision day. He went into Roy's office to see which of us formerly under his control were to be kept on or released. Steve had worked with us all for the last eight or nine years and knew us better than anyone else at the club.

The message from the manager when I had my meeting was, 'You've done all right, we need to see more, but you've got another year.' That was it, short and sweet.

The message from Steve the following day was, 'They were thinking of releasing you. I told them to be patient and give you time.' I knew Steve had probably saved me and I also knew if I wanted to survive I had to do better. This was Liverpool and whether I had been there ten years or not there was no sentiment: you were either good enough or you weren't.

I agreed another year's contract on £350 a week and the same signing-on fee. There was to be no breaking of the bank to secure my signature for another year.

During the summer there was a major change as for the first time Liverpool appointed joint managers, with Frenchman Gérard Houllier coming in to work alongside Roy Evans. There were massive changes within the youth system as well as Liverpool becoming the first club to open a football academy, a brand-new facility just outside the City in Kirkby. The only immediate issue was that it wouldn't be ready to be used until October.

The big problem for me was that Liverpool had made a lot of new signings that summer and there was now a big squad at Melwood and, rightly or wrongly, the new management had decided that the three young pros who had been kept on from the previous year (me, Tommy Culshaw and Danny Williams) were not to train at Melwood and would instead be training with the new first-year pros and the YTS lads.

It wasn't a great welcome back for pre-season, but at least I knew I would be working with H, Steve and Dave again who all rated me as a player. With the new academy facility in Kirkby not yet ready, we were to train at Liverpool Hope University in Aigburth for the first few months of the season and it was heart-breaking to drive past Melwood every morning to get there.

Pre-season went as well as could be expected and the three of us were invited to Melwood occasionally to train with the first-team.

However, once the season began, we were in a bizarre situation. The traditional A and B team leagues had been scrapped and replaced with new under-17 and under-19 leagues, which meant that at 19 we were all too old to play for these teams and at Melwood Gérard Houllier had decided that the first-team players who weren't starting would all play for the reserves, so none of us even made it on to the bench there.

For six weeks we trained all week and had no match to look forward to. It was a crazy situation for any player, but particularly young players trying to make their way in the game.

At the time I had most Sundays off, and I would go and watch my brother play for his Sunday side – the Liverpool Supporters' Club team. After six weeks of not having a game and being totally fed up with my situation, I convinced the manager Les Lawson to throw me on when one of the lads picked up an injury.

Looking back, it was absolute madness. If I had got injured I would have been in serious trouble and I certainly had to hurdle a few tackles, but at least I got my first game and goal of the season!

That week I was told to report to Melwood for a behind-closed doors fixture against Blackburn. We had a strong squad made up of players who hadn't been starting and those coming back from injury, with Brad Friedel, Carra, Dom Matteo, David Thompson, Neil Ruddock and Øyvind Leonhardsen all playing.

Both the senior managers were there, and the game was taken by the new first-team coach Patrice Bergues, who I really liked.

I was on the left wing and despite having not played for so long, other than my 20-minute guest appearance for the supporters' club, I felt sharp and scored once in a 2-1 win.

The following week we played against Wrexham, who included a lot of their first-team players, and I scored twice and made two for the returning Robbie Fowler in an 8-1 win.

When I arrived at Liverpool Hope University for training the following day Dave Shannon asked me how the game had gone.

'Yeah, good,' I replied. 'I did well, scored a couple and felt sharp.'

'Well, we were speaking to the first-team staff at Anfield last night and both Patrice and Gérard Houllier said you were the best player on the pitch,' Dave said to me.

I was delighted to hear that; it gave my confidence a massive boost and I felt that all my hard work in the summer was beginning to pay off – or maybe Gérard Houllier had been on a recent scouting mission to Botanic Park near Wavertree to watch the supporters' club on a Sunday morning.

After the games against Blackburn and Wrexham I was invited to Melwood quite often to train along with two other younger players, Stephen Wright and Steven Gerrard. Stevie G in particular was causing quite a stir among the first-team group every time he trained with them.

In the November of that season Houllier was left in sole charge as Roy Evans had left. I wasn't at Melwood enough to know everything but when I was it was a bit awkward with Roy called 'Gaffer' and Gérard called 'Boss'. I never really knew who to speak to when I wanted to talk to the manager and there was no way that the two men, with the distinguished coaching careers they'd had, were ever going to take a back seat to the other.

With the first-team struggling on the pitch there was only ever going to be one fall guy and unfortunately it was Roy, who only a couple of seasons earlier had come close to managing Liverpool to the Premier League title.

I started to become a regular in the reserves leading up to Christmas and I was in good form and training with the first-team a couple of days a week.

I enjoyed the training, with Houllier leading the tactical side and Patrice and Sammy Lee taking the other part of the sessions.

Phil Thompson had also come in as assistant manager, but if Patrice was good cop among the players then Thommo was most definitely bad cop. He would roar at the players and was certainly the motivator. He was exactly what you see on the television these days. At times he wasn't the most popular member of staff, but he wouldn't have cared. He was Liverpool through and through and didn't care who he upset.

His only concern was trying to take Liverpool back to the top, where they had been in his playing days. He wore his heart on his sleeve and played a big part in helping the club challenge for honours again; his passion was evident.

I was playing with a lot of confidence in games, and it was one of those spells where I felt I could play against anyone.

In early January we had a reserve team game at home to Leicester City which we won 2-1. I scored a late winner, and the manager was full of praise for me and told me to report to Melwood instead of the university in the morning and to go to his office for a chat when I got there. Although I was someone who always thought the glass was half empty, even I thought this had to be good news. And it was.

He told me he had been really impressed with me over the last few months and that he felt I was ready to train with the first-team permanently and be part of the squad. On top of that he wanted to offer me a new contract, another two years on top of the half a season I had left. I was buzzing. It was a massive boost for the manager to show how much he rated me.

I had no agent in those days; I hardly needed one on £350 a week did I? I had a meeting with chief executive Peter Robinson at Anfield a few days later and signed a new two-year contract, doubling my wages, with increases in the following two seasons, and also received a £30,000 signing-on fee split over three payments over the length of the contract.

I finally felt like a Liverpool player when moving into the first-team dressing room for the first time. My peg in the changing room was in between David James and Stéphane Henchoz. You could not get two more different characters. Steph was like me, very quiet and he would say a polite hello to everyone when he came in in the morning, whereas Jamo would come bouncing in larger than life telling us he had seen aliens landing in his garden the night before.

It was around this time that the manager signed a fellow Frenchman, Jean-Michel Ferri. It was an odd transfer. He was a midfielder in his early 30s and was never going to play ahead of any of those already in the squad and, with Steven Gerrard about to make his breakthrough, it just didn't add up.

He was very professional, played with us in the reserves and always gave his all, but he gave the impression of being the eyes and ears in the dressing room that Houllier wanted.

He also spoke very good English and any plans that some of the players may have occasionally made for a night out always seemed to get back to the manager that particular season. It was very clever of Houllier, who I'm sure in his first season wanted to know the ins and outs of all the players. However he had probably underestimated how streetwise the players in that dressing room were, especially the Scouse lads, and there were a few wild goose chases spoken about within earshot of Ferri as the players quickly worked him out.

The rest of the season for me went really well as I scored regularly for the reserves. I was in good form and the manager kept hinting to me privately that I might be involved in the first-team squad before the season ended, but it just didn't happen. I was a bit disappointed by that.

I knew that, while I was playing with this level of confidence, I would have relished the chance of 20 minutes in an end-of-season game. I didn't understand the logic of the likes of Sean Dundee being on the bench when it was clear he had no future at the club.

'Croc', as he was known, was a lovely fella but he simply did not help himself from the minute he arrived that summer. He was miles off the pace, both in training and games, and looked overweight, and his yellow Porsche didn't half stand out in the McDonald's drive-thru on Edge Lane!

At that time I was the next forward in line behind him and the way I was playing in the reserves I deserved a place on the bench more than he did in the final few games of that season, especially when he had no future, but with the club looking to recoup a few million quid for him in the summer he was kept in the first-team picture.

My first full season in the first-team squad was 1999/2000. The club had backed the manager and he had made some big signings, bringing in Sami Hyypiä, Titi Camara, Erik Meijer, Vladimír Šmicer and Sander Westerveld. Of those, Camara and big Erik were out-and-out strikers, Šmicer could play up there too if necessary and the club already had Karl-Heinz Riedle, a German World Cup winner, and Patrik Berger.

Add those to the goalscoring masterclasses of Robbie Fowler and Michael Owen and it was clear it would be a tough squad to break in to.

That pre-season we went to Switzerland for ten days, which was different to what the players were used to. We were in the Swiss mountains in the middle of nowhere and we would train three times a day.

At 7am we would go to the training pitches for the long-distance running and then it would be back to the hotel for breakfast and a rest. At 11am we would be in the gym doing individual weights programmes, then it was more food and a sleep in the afternoon, and then at 5pm we would train with the football with a lot of high intensity work.

By the end of the ten days I felt as fit as I had ever done. With the new signings the club was on the way up and we were strengthened further as Didi Hamann arrived on the last day of the trip as another high-profile transfer.

The season started as the previous one ended with me full of confidence and playing well. The manager again insisted that those first-team players not starting in the Premier League would play in the reserves and that suited me. It meant I was playing with quality every game and that could only improve me.

I formed a great partnership with Erik Meijer. He was a real character, never quiet, always had an opinion, loved working hard and was a big help passing on advice to the younger players.

He only played a handful of first-team games, but the Kop loved him. You couldn't help but like big Erik off the pitch either, he had no filter and said whatever was on his mind, not really bothered if he upset someone. He always kept us entertained and was great to have in the dressing room.

He was the type of striker I loved to play alongside. He was a giant of a man with a real presence. He held the ball up, won headers, took the hits and I would make my runs off him and we complimented each other really well, making goals for one another.

My continued good form for the reserves made me believe I had a chance to play for the first-team in some of the cup competitions and I was rewarded by being named in the squad for the second leg of the League Cup game against Hull City at Anfield.

We were leading 5-1 from the first leg and when Phil Thompson came around on the Monday asking what I wanted as my pre-match meal the following day I knew I was in. The kit man Graham gave me a shout after training to show me my first-team shirt. NEWBY with the number 32 on the back. I was hoping the following day I would be making my debut for Liverpool.

I was named as one of the subs in the team meeting on the Tuesday afternoon, with the line-up being strong despite a lot of players being rested.

Brad Friedel, Stéphane Henchoz, Rigobert Song, Steve Staunton, Danny Murphy, David Thompson, Patrik Berger and Karl Heinz-Riedle all started. I got the call to warm up midway through the second half and with 25 minutes to go I got the nod from the manager to make my debut for Liverpool.

I was to replace Henchoz and with a slight reorganisation of the team I went to the right-hand side of midfield. It was 2-2 at the time with fellow young debutant Layton Maxwell having scored our second goal.

Riedle put us back in front shortly after I went on and with us having most of the ball, I got plenty of touches and grew in confidence.

In the last minute I received a pass from David Thompson on the touchline about 20 yards out and had space to run at the full-back. I dropped my shoulder and skipped past him getting to the byline at the Kop end and stood up a perfect cross to the back post which Riedle headed home for his farewell goal for the club.

I was really pleased with how my debut had gone. We had won 4-2 and I had made a goal.

I remember Danny Murphy and 'Stan' Staunton congratulating me in the dressing room on making my debut and creating a goal. It was the start of a couple of months of being in the first-team matchday squad most weeks. I would often be 17th man with only five subs allowed those days, but at least it showed I was impressing the manager enough to be in his thoughts.

My next taste of being on the bench was in early December in the FA Cup away at Huddersfield Town. It was a game live on the television. Huddersfield were flying high in the league below and hoping for an upset.

The match went to plan for us with Titi Camara giving us a first-half lead and our second goal coming from Dom Matteo in a 2-0 win. I made my second appearance from the bench in the final ten minutes and replaced Steven Gerrard, again on the right of midfield.

I was next in the squad for the Boxing Day fixture away at Newcastle United. We trained at Melwood on Christmas Day morning and then were allowed home to see the family for a few hours before leaving from Anfield late afternoon for the north-east.

I was rooming with Frenchman Djimi Traore who had only signed a few months previously. The manager had banned the French players from speaking their own language around the training ground to help them improve their English, but so far Djimi only knew a few words of and most of them were swear words so I don't think he had been turning up to his English lessons after training.

Christmas night spent in a hotel with Djimi was a bit different to what I was used to, but I took charge of the television remote and treated my roomie to the *Royle Family* Christmas special. Djimi's quizzical looks towards me as he listened to Ricky Tomlinson moan at his mother-in-law for the next hour made me realise that Jim Royle and Nana clearly weren't popular television characters back in Paris!

I didn't make the bench the following day as Houllier went with an extra defender with the game being away from home and we drew 2-2, with Michael Owen scoring both at a ground where he always seemed to net.

I made my third substitute appearance as we were knocked out of the FA Cup at home to Blackburn and we then used the free weekend, when the next round was played, to fly to Malta for four days of training in some warmer weather.

The only problem was that when we got off the plane and headed straight to the national stadium that evening, all the pitches were waterlogged due to the amount of rain that had fallen over the previous few days.

The rule while in Malta was no drinking at all, but a few of the lads thought it would be a disappointment if they went home without sampling the local nightlife and, having been to Malta a few times on holiday myself, I told them that there were a few good clubs in St Julian's which was very close to our hotel.

So on the last night four or five of the lads sneaked out despite us needing to be on the team coach to leave for the airport at 5.30am the following day. At about five o'clock Stig Bjørnebye, who I was rooming with, was waking me up telling me to come out to the balcony. As we looked down at the pool we could see a few of the lads jumping over sun loungers trying to get back into the hotel without being seen.

The worse for wear on the local Maltese lager, they were pretending to be in the army using their fingers as guns crouching behind the sun beds, giving each other the 'all clear, let's go' hand signals in a bid to make it home. They had to be quick because we were leaving for our flight back to Manchester half an hour later.

The players in question, though, were regretting their decision to go out when our flight home hit turbulence on the way back into Manchester,. It was so bad that it made the papers the next day, and there were a few green faces as we came in to land.

On returning from Malta I was in the squad for the away trip to Watford, which we won 3-2, and the following week we faced Middlesbrough at Anfield in the Premier League and I was named as a sub for the first time in the Premier League.

Michael Owen picked up an injury in the first half and was replaced by Erik Meijer, so I was the only forward player left on the bench, and with 25 minutes left I got the call to replace Vladimír Šmicer on the right-hand side of midfield. I desperately wanted to play up front, which was more natural to me, but I was about to play in the Premier League for Liverpool, the team I had supported all my life.

I looked up at the Kop as I waited with the linesman knowing that my dad and my brother were watching from our season tickets in block 206. It was an amazing feeling hearing the roar of encouragement from the Anfield crowd of over 44,000 as I ran on to take my place near the Centenary Stand.

Curtis Fleming was playing at left-back for the visitors and I knew he was fast, so I had to move the ball quickly. As soon as I went on Sami Hyypiä played a pass in to me and I took a touch and played it inside to Didi Hamann. The first thing I had done had been positive and I wanted to try and make an impact. I got it back off Didi and Paul Ince, who had been at Liverpool until earlier that season, smashed into me with a late tackle – and the crowd roared their disproval. Ince grinned at me as he half-picked me up as if to say, 'Welcome to the game.'

In the end the game finished 0-0 and I hadn't had as much of the ball as I'd wanted. We started playing longer, looking to feed off big Erik, but they had Gary Pallister at the back and he dealt with it comfortably.

Still, I had made my debut in the Premier League at Anfield against the likes of Pallister, Ince and Juninho. It was a dream come true and something I look back on with great pride. It wasn't the highlight of my career but is something that I'm very proud of. I wanted more than one Premier League appearance with Liverpool, though, but that never happened.

The following week I was again on the bench for the home game against Leeds, who were challenging for the title that season. The atmosphere was absolutely electric with it being 1-1 going into the last 20 minutes. I would have loved to have got on against such opposition but I don't think the manager had the confidence to throw me on in such a big game.

Patrik Berger and Danny Murphy both scored screamers at the Kop end late on to give us a 3-1 win and the dressing room was absolutely bouncing.

Little did I know then, however, that the Leeds game would be the last time I would be in the first-team matchday squad for Liverpool.

Players like Fowler, Owen and Camara were all returning from injury and the club had just spent £11m on Emile Heskey, who was a perfect fit in the dressing room and was a massively underrated player for us.

I kept playing well and scoring for the reserves which was all I could do. I got two at home to Blackburn in a 3-3 draw, where I partnered Robbie Fowler up front, another two in a 6-2 win at Barnsley and a last-minute goal at home to Aston Villa in another victory.

It was in this game against Villa that Dario Gradi saw me play and the next day Gérard Houllier called me in to his office to tell me that Championship side Crewe Alexandra wanted to take me on loan for a month and he felt it would benefit me to go and play regular first-team games at that level.

I agreed and was to join one of my Liverpool team-mates, Stephen Wright, who was already on loan at Gresty Road. So for the next month I was to get my first taste of football away from what I had always known.

2

It was like starting a new school

I WAS nervous. I was a quiet lad anyway and it was my first spell away from Liverpool, so it was the unknown. I met the manager, had a brief chat with him and then made my way into the dressing room.

The first-team-mate I met was Mancunian Colin Little who greeted me with, 'All right mate, you don't want to buy a watch do you? Comes boxed and everything.' Col was the man in Crewe's dressing room who could get you anything. There was one at every club, I would come to learn over the years.

Paul Tait, a Geordie lad who had come through Everton's youth system, answered him before I could. 'Fuckin hell, Col, let him get through the door first, hey.'

Football changing rooms are all very similar and you quickly work out who the leaders and main characters are, and there were some lively personalities at Crewe.

Training was short and sweet the day before a game at Crewe and I was hoping to start the following day at home to Norwich City. I did, on the right-hand side of midfield, where Gradi had seen me play for Liverpool reserves, something that would ultimately work against me. The game itself started well enough as I was involved in the move which saw Neil Sorvel score the only goal after just five minutes – but after that I had a nightmare.

I could not have played any worse if I had tried to. The harder I tried the worse I got. I was eventually put out of my misery after about 70 minutes and Gradi was probably ready to send me back to Liverpool that night!

I remember that game for one other incident too. The man who replaced me was Rob Hulse, who went on to have a very good career in the Premier League and Championship. That day it was also his debut for Crewe. He had 20 minutes to impress but only lasted for 15.

As Norwich pushed forward searching for an equaliser, leaving gaps at the back, Hulse did well to find himself one-on-one with their goalkeeper twice in very quick succession with the chance to kill the game off. When the keeper denied him for the second time Gradi ran from the dugout until he was a yard on the pitch screaming, 'Get him off!'

I thought he was just being a normal manager screaming at a player in frustration for missing a chance, but 30 seconds later Hulse's number was up on the board and he was back sat on the bench he had just left – looking a bit confused.

It was some debut for a young lad and Gradi didn't seem the type of manager who was going to give players much support. I couldn't wait to get out of the ground. I was annoyed with myself and had let myself down with my performance and couldn't understand where it had come from when I'd been playing with such confidence back at Liverpool.

We had another home game at Gresty Road only three days later, a derby against local rivals Port Vale under the lights, but to be honest I wasn't expecting to start. Fortunately I was named in the line-up, again on the right, and I was determined not to waste this opportunity.

As we were in the dressing room waiting to go and line up in the tunnel I noticed the physio talking to Rodney Jack, who was Crewe's record signing and top striker. He had been away on international duty and had only just returned to the country that morning so he wasn't involved in the game. I saw him nod towards me and ask the physio what I was like. The physio shook his head and screwed up his face, obviously referring to Saturday's performance. To be fair he could have been a lot harsher!

However, as we ran out a minute or so later, I was still fuming about the physio and knew I had something to prove.

I must have been pissed off because within 30 seconds of the kick-off I flew into a tackle with the Port Vale left-back, leaving him on the floor. I hardly ever tackled and when I did, I never took anyone down, so the physio must have got to me more than I thought.

I went on to have a really good game and was a constant threat to Port Vale all night as we won 2-1 with goals from two quality players, Colin Cramb and Kenny Lunt. I even got a 'well done' off Dario Gradi on the way back to the dressing room after the game and I was hoping that somewhere Rodney Jack was saying to the physio, 'You told me he was useless!'

We had the day off the following day, so I went into Melwood for a warm-down and Sammy Lee came over to say well done as him and Phil Thompson had been at the match. If Sammy was telling me that I'd played well I must have done, as he wasn't one for giving out compliments unless he had to.

That was something I liked about Sammy. He would tell it how he saw it no matter who you were. If you weren't at it, he would tell you whether you were a young pro or a superstar. I don't think Sammy was my biggest fan in my first year as a pro at Liverpool but I would like to think that as time went on, he recognised I worked extremely hard in every game that I played for the club and that I did enough to convince him that I could make a living out of the game – even if it wasn't at Premier League level.

Back at Crewe our next game was on the Sunday away at Blackburn's Ewood Park, on Sky. Blackburn had fallen out of the Premier League but still had quality players such as Damien Duff,

David Dunn, Ashley Ward and Christian Dailly, who all played in the top flight for years.

I had always enjoyed playing at Ewood Park in the reserves and with the game on the television and a good crowd expected it was set to be a decent occasion. After my performance against Port Vale I had no concerns about not being in the starting line-up, but with Rodney Jack returning to the team I was moved to the left.

I was comfortable with both feet and enjoyed playing on the left more as I could cut in on my right foot. There was also the added bonus of not having to chase Damien Duff if I played on the left, so I was more than happy to be on the opposite wing to him.

The way that Gradi set his team up would suit the big pitch at Blackburn and there would be plenty of space for us to play. The only problem was that there was also space for Duff to run into and he could shift.

We looked a real threat going forward with Cramby and Mark Rivers, who were both intelligent footballers, playing up front, with the pace of Jack and myself in wide areas and the creativity of Lunt and Sorvel in central midfield.

But it was almost like a school match. You attack, we attack. The only thing missing was fly keepers. It was the most open match I ever played in.

I still hadn't scored a first-team goal, but up against the ageing Simon Grayson, who was at right-back, I fancied my chances of getting at him with my pace. I started the game well, flying past him a couple of times and getting dangerous crosses into the box, and it was obvious from the shouts coming from their bench that they saw me as a real threat.

Midway through the first half I thought my first senior goal had arrived when Blackburn only half-cleared a cross, and the ball dropped to the edge of the box. I caught it perfectly on the half-volley and it flew towards the bottom corner.

Any footballer knows when they couldn't have struck a ball any sweeter and this was one of those times, but somehow Alan

Kelly pulled off an unbelievable save with the ball cannoning off his wrist and over the bar.

I was already about to start my celebration. If I had mis-kicked it the ball would probably have trickled in.

After that, for the next 60 minutes, it was like the Alamo. We got absolutely battered and it was the most one-sided game I was ever involved in, even ones that I've lost comfortably.

The stats on the television showed that Blackburn had 33 shots with over 20 on target. Our keeper, the experienced Australian Jason Kearton, had the game of his life. He wasn't just making saves, every one of them was an absolute worldie.

At one stage we were about to defend a corner after another unbelievable save and players from both sides were laughing with each other about how the game was still 0-0. Duff alone could have scored about six if it hadn't been for Kearton.

However, with nine minutes left the unthinkable happened and we took the lead. A break away was finished by Colin Cramb and, although we had to hang on at the end, Blackburn were never going to score. It was just one of those days when they could have played all day and still drawn a blank.

Cramby summed it up when we got back into a jubilant dressing room with his comment, 'I think we bossed it to be honest boys,' with his usual Scottish humour. Even the manager had to laugh.

I was personally delighted with my own performance. I had been a threat going forward and had dug in and defended in the second half. I was also loving playing in games that meant something rather than reserve team matches. We now had a week to prepare for a home fixture with Portsmouth and a few of us needed a week to recover from the trenches we had dug just outside our own penalty area at Ewood Park.

Portsmouth came with a great following, which created a lively atmosphere, but we had used up all our luck at Blackburn and were beaten 3-1.

I had again played well on the left and was beginning to feel more at home with every game I played in the Championship. I suffered a dead leg late on after I got a knee in the thigh off big centre-back Darren Moore. Anyone who has seen him play will tell you he is not only six feet tall but also about six feet wide and pure muscle, and I knew the dead leg wasn't going to be one I could shake off easily.

Our next game was that Tuesday away at Molineux against Wolves and on the Monday, I was still hobbling and couldn't bend my leg properly. I didn't train that day either, but the physio got stuck into the bruising and I told the manager I'd be fit to play.

In my career I didn't miss a game through niggly injuries; it had to be something where there was no way I could play. At times I was probably foolish to play with certain injuries but I hated missing matches out of fear of not getting back in the team when I had worked hard to get in, and Wolves was one of those times where I definitely made the wrong decision to declare myself fit.

My rule was always if I could sprint, no matter how painful it was, then I could play. My pace was my biggest attribute so if the injury wasn't affecting how quickly I could run I would play.

The only problem against Wolves was that Australian international Kevin Muscat was their right-back. I remember once reading a quote by Peter Crouch saying the only footballer to ever scare him was Muscat. That makes two of us, Crouchy.

Muscat kicked me up in the air all night and when I landed, he would kick me up in the air again. He may as well have been playing Aussie rules.

Truth be told, he was the type of defender I hated playing against. He was quick, strong and physical and I let him intimidate me and mentally I wasn't strong enough to deal with him.

I had been playing so well leading up to that game, but I was poor that night and rightly found myself dragged off after 65 minutes and on the end of a bit of stick from Gradi.

I was probably only about 70 per cent fit, but I wasn't using that as an excuse. I had been poor, was rightly subbed and we deservedly lost 2-0.

I had two matches of my loan spell left, against Huddersfield and Nottingham Forest, and we would lose them both without scoring or, in fact, looking remotely like scoring.

I had played every game wide on either side of midfield and of course I know Gradi had seen me play in that position for Liverpool reserves and had signed me to play there for Crewe, but I was a centre-forward and believed I could play there at Championship level.

After the Huddersfield game the manager said to the press that he needed a forward with pace to get behind the opposition as the team weren't scoring enough goals. I was left out of the team and was an unused sub, which strictly speaking I couldn't argue with after my performance at Wolves. So on the Monday I went to see him, we had a chat and I reminded him that I was a centre-forward and had the pace to stretch opposition defences.

I wasn't expecting him to jump up and shout 'the saviour is here', but I just wanted to plant the seed in his mind that I was a centre-forward and was at my best there. The conversation was amicable and there were certainly no demands from me that either I play up front or I didn't want to play at all.

Yet when I got to the training ground on Friday morning someone showed me the *Daily Star* where Gradi said that he was not extending my loan spell as he wasn't having me dictate what position I played. To say I wasn't happy was an understatement. In those days I was quiet, probably too quiet for my own good, but straight away I went to his office with the paper.

'What's all that about?' I asked him, shoving the paper towards him.

He read the article quickly before looking at me with a smile telling me that he had been misquoted.

'Bollocks,' I said back at him. 'All I did was tell you I was a centre-forward. I haven't demanded to play anywhere.'

He refused to accept he had said anything like that, but the story could only have come from our conversation and I thought it was really poor from such an experienced manager.

He could have simply told the truth and said he wasn't extending my loan spell as he personally didn't think I'd had enough of an impact. There was no need for him to twist a private conversation to try and make me out to be some kind of big-time Charlie from a Premier League club.

In my opinion he got it massively wrong in how he dealt with the situation by going to the press and saying what he said, but in the month that I spent at Crewe that was how Gradi came across, as someone who was never wrong and to challenge him or even offer an opinion of your own was something that wasn't allowed in his mind.

Even to this day I still don't understand why he felt the need to twist a conversation and put it in the press.

I left Crewe at the end of that week after playing ten minutes on the right of midfield as we lost 3-0 at home to Nottingham Forest. I said my goodbyes to the players after the game, but I made no attempt to find the manager and wish him all the best. We simply hadn't seen eye to eye in the time I was at the club and by the end of the month I had very little respect for Gradi.

My first loan spell had come to an end and had proved to be a massive learning experience. In three of the games, against Port Vale, Blackburn Rovers and Portsmouth, I had performed very well, but I was disappointed with how it had all ended.

The relationship between the two clubs became strained for a while after that as I know the Liverpool staff at Melwood were not happy with how I had been portrayed.

The *Daily Post* reported on the incident during the week, saying, 'Liverpool striker Jon Newby's loan spell at Crewe has been soured by a disagreement with the First Division side's manager Dario Gradi.

'The 21 year-old will return to Liverpool on Monday on the day his one-month loan spell at Gresty Road was originally scheduled to end.

'But Gradi has hit out at the departing Newby, who allegedly refused his request to play as a winger.

'Gradi rapped, "He has suddenly decided he can't play as a winger. He couldn't handle what I wanted him to do and has decided to go back to Liverpool."

'Gradi's outburst against the mild-mannered youngster will astonish Liverpool officials. Newby is a popular figure at Anfield and currently leads the reserves' scoring charts with 11 goals in 16 appearances.'

I returned to Melwood for the final few weeks of the season and scored in the last reserve game against Everton at Anfield, which was always nice. We won the Premier Reserve League title that season and I finished as the top goal scorer with 13 goals in 19 games.

It had been an eventful season. I had made my debut for Liverpool, played in the Premier League, and had my first loan spell away from the club, playing in the Championship, but I was heading into the final year of my contract and I knew I had some big decisions to make.

3

I wasn't emotional about leaving Liverpool

THE 2000/01 season started much the same as the previous one with ten days away in the Swiss mountains for a pre-season training camp. The big signings in the summer were Christian Ziege and Nick Barmby with the latter having seen the light and moved across Stanley Park from rivals Everton.

The third major transfer, and something of a surprise, was Gary McAllister, but he turned out to be probably the signing of the season and became a massively important player for the club.

As younger players we learnt an awful lot from him. His attitude in training was second to none and his fitness levels in pre-season were up there alongside the best in the squad. He was like a hungry kid trying to make his way in the game.

During that summer I met with an agent through my old Liverpool team-mate Mark Wright. It wasn't about money, it was more about the fact I thought I would soon need someone who had a lot of contacts at other clubs as I entered the last year of my contract.

I instantly liked Scotsman George Urquhart, who had a couple of big players in his stable, and I signed a deal with him as my first and only agent in my career should I need one.

As the new signings settled in and there was a fully fit squad, Gérard Houllier told me he was happy for me to go out on loan again should any offers come in. I knew there was a bit of interest in me and George rang me to say Neil Warnock was very interested in taking me to Sheffield United who, like Crewe, were in the Championship.

Compared to Crewe the Blades were a massive club and I liked what Warnock had said on the phone so travelled to Bramall Lane to sign in the last week of pre-season. I met him and his assistant Kevin Blackwell, who I liked immediately, got the contracts signed and the manager then told me he would give me a lift to the training ground.

As we walked out of reception at Bramall Lane, I noticed a bright red Ferrari in the car park. Warnock pressed the keys to open it. The doors opened upwards instead of out and it was like getting into a spaceship. If there was ever someone who didn't look right driving a Ferrari it had to be Neil Warnock. You could pick a manager from any club in the world and he surely had to be the man least suited to driving that car.

I wasn't complaining about being driven to training in it, even though the seats were that low it felt like you were lying on the floor.

It wasn't actually his. Keith Curle, Sheffield United's captain, had let him drive it for the morning – or had been told he was letting him drive it, knowing the manager!

Training had already started by the time I arrived, and I joined in the match at the end and felt sharp having had a good pre-season with Liverpool.

The two main forwards at the club were Marcus Bent and veteran David 'Ned' Kelly, who had scored goals at every level he had played at. He was a massive personality and character, just the type any manager wants in the dressing room.

With a midfield four of Paul Devlin, Curtis Woodhouse, Michael Brown and Bruno Ribeiro the club wasn't short of firepower. The last pre-season game was at Rotherham, where notorious centre-half Guy Branston kicked me from start to finish, but at least he picked me up with a smile every time he flattened me.

We won 2-1 and I played the full 90 minutes up front, making the winner with a great run and cross for Nic Weber to head home.

I lived in the Marriott hotel in Sheffield while I was on loan and hotel life could be very boring, especially if you had finished training by 1pm.

The hotel was used by many away teams and our opening-day fixture was a home game with Portsmouth, who at the time were managed by Tony Pulis, and they were staying there too. No matter where I bumped into Pulis on that Friday and Saturday, whether it was in the corridor, dining room or the gardens, he had that trademark baseball cap on!

The game itself was played in glorious sunshine and even though, as expected, Warnock opted to start with Bent and Ned up front, I was confident I would get on in the game.

Paul Devlin gave us the lead from the penalty spot in the first half, but Warnock wasn't particularly happy with the team at half-time and wasn't shy at letting them know.

I got the nod to go on after an hour and replaced Ned and did really well. We won 2-0, backed by a very vocal Bramall Lane crowd who knew how to create an atmosphere. It was a good start to the season for the team and me personally.

I was due to start in midweek in the League Cup against Lincoln City and I felt it would be a real chance to get my first senior goal against League 2 opposition – especially as I was full of confidence after my role in the opening-day win.

The night before our game Liverpool were playing away at Arsenal in the Premier League, which I watched in my hotel room, and they had both Gary McAllister and Didi Hamann sent off.

I didn't think that would affect my situation particularly with neither of them playing in the same position as I did, but Sheffield

United received a call from Liverpool on the morning of our game to say I was no longer allowed to play in the cup in case I was needed in that competition for Liverpool later in the season. I was absolutely gutted; how McAllister and Hamann being sent off influenced that decision I'll never know.

I was even more frustrated that night when Sheffield United picked Lincoln off at will, winning 6-1. Neither of the centre-backs were quick and it would have been the perfect match for me to play in. Little pieces of bad luck like this, that were totally out of my hands, affected parts of my career.

Not having scored a senior goal yet was playing on my mind massively. Being a player who relied so heavily on confidence, a goal against Lincoln would have given me a massive boost and hopefully I could have kicked on from there.

There was no guarantee I would have scored against Lincoln but with us netting six I would definitely have had opportunities to open my account with how many chances we created in the game.

The League Cup that season for Sheffield United was remembered for another reason – the bust up between Paul Devlin and Marcus Bent on the pitch in a later round against Colchester United, over Dev not giving Bent a tap-in late in the game with us already 3-0 up. They were both excellent players and massive for Sheffield United, but both could be hot-headed at times and were really strong characters.

Warnock attempted to diffuse the situation by taking Bent off straight away. When we got down to the dressing room, however, it was clear that neither of them was going to back down from the argument on the pitch and a massive fight broke out with most of the other players jumping in trying to separate them.

Warnock, however, wasn't bothered by it in the slightest and was jumping up and down like he was in the front row of a boxing match. It was made even more surreal by Bent being naked the whole time having just got out of the shower!

It was all forgotten about a few days later as they lined up alongside each other in an away win at Crystal Palace, where Bent got the winner, assisted by Devlin.

As well as Devlin and Bent there were some massive personalities in that squad and plenty of experience. Simon Tracey, part of the infamous Wimbledon Crazy Gang, was in goal, my Dutch room-mate Gus Uhlenbeek was at right-back with Wayne Quinn, who was sold to Newcastle, at left-back. Experienced pair Keith Curle and Georges Santos were the centre-backs.

Georges was an absolute giant, softly spoken off the pitch but wanted to kill you on it. Warnock just wanted him to head it and kick it.

'Fuck off with all that fancy stuff, Georges, I pay you to defend,' was the manager's regular shout at half-time and Georges would look at him arms outstretched and say, 'But Gaffer, I can play.'

I'm sure Georges had a bonus in his contract that paid him a few quid if he nutmegged people. He wasn't happy if he came off the pitch and he hadn't 'megged' someone. In training he would constantly be trying it and would run off laughing when he succeeded.

I was on the receiving end and he never let you forget it. The unwritten rule in football is if you get nutmegged in training then the player who did it knows that the next time he is on the ball his victim is going to give him a kick as if to say, 'Oi, don't do that again.' Nobody ever tried to kick Georges, though. He would just kick you back five times as hard!

As well as Devlin, who had real quality, the midfield was made up of ex-Manchester City player Michael Brown, who was a very talented player, with Curtis Woodhouse, who was one of the funniest lads I ever met in football alongside him, and then either Bobby Ford, a very underrated player, or ex-Leeds man Bruno Ribeiro in the last midfield spot.

With Bent and David Kelly up front and the likes of Shaun Murphy, Lee Sandford and Laurent D'Jaffo also in the squad it was a group of tough players. There was a real steel about the squad and with Phil Jagielka and Nick Montgomery on the bench showing their quality the future looked good for the club.

As the matches went by, I was still only getting 20 minutes in most games which was frustrating, and due to me not being able to play in the League Cup I had to watch from the stand as we took on bitter rivals Sheffield Wednesday at Hillsborough for a 2-1 defeat in what was a toxic atmosphere. There seemed genuine hatred between the two sets of fans.

I eventually got my first start away at Birmingham City at St Andrew's. I was playing on the left of midfield and did well. It was the closest I had come to my first goal, with Birmingham keeper Ian Bennett making a great save to deny me. It was becoming a weight on my shoulders trying to get my first senior goal and I was going into games with it playing on my mind.

I wasn't finishing badly or snatching at chances, and I was scoring a lot of goals for the Blades' reserves. I had just been unfortunate that for both Crewe and Sheffield United, opposition goalkeepers had pulled off two unbelievable saves.

We undeservedly lost 1-0 at Birmingham but I kept my place for the next game a few days later away at Wolves, which meant a reunion with Kevin Muscat.

I struggled against him again, emphasising that mentally I wasn't tough enough and that I had to improve my mindset to play against players like him. Strangely enough he kicked me all over the place again and elbowed me in the face off the ball, but I was the one booked for dissent for arguing with the ref over the elbow.

Neil Warnock had a few things to say about Muscat's performance in the press and that was something I liked about the manager. He always looked after his players.

From the outside a lot of fans don't like Warnock and if you haven't worked with him I can understand why, but on the inside, he creates a siege mentality and makes you feel like it's 'us against the world'.

He is hard and ruthless with his players, but he also knew when to put an arm around them. I always found him very fair and really enjoyed working with him. He certainly had the respect of all his players at Sheffield United.

He was different in the way he did certain things and we even went to watch the video of a defeat at Preston in the front room of his house one afternoon with half of us sat on the floor, but as the years have gone by, he has got results and promotions and done a good job at nearly every club he has managed.

Yes, he thrives on controversy at times, but he does it, in my opinion, because he thinks it will benefit his club. Love him or hate him, he loves football and knows how to win.

After the two games in the Midlands, we had no fixture during international week in early October and the manager took us to La Manga in Spain for a few days of warm-weather training. It certainly wasn't warm at six o'clock in the morning in the outdoor pool though!

Warnock would have the physios knock us up early every morning and we would have to do ten lengths in the pool with ten press-ups at poolside after each one.

If he wasn't happy with your press-ups he or Kevin Blackwell would throw you back in the pool for an extra length, which was about every three lengths no matter how good your press-up form was. It was good for team spirit but the walk back to the apartments freezing to death wasn't much fun with the manager laughing his head off behind us.

There were only a couple of weeks left of my three-month loan spell so I had a good chat with Gérard Houllier, and it was agreed that we wouldn't extend it when it came to an end.

If I was only playing 20 minutes or so each game in the first-team it seemed pointless staying to play in the reserves when I could be back at Anfield in Liverpool's second string. He understood that and both Neil and Kevin were good footballing people to work with.

The final two games were away at Wimbledon at Selhurst Park and at home to Gillingham. At Wimbledon I suffered one of those moments that every footballer dreads – I was subbed on and off in the same game. I went on after 20 minutes due to an injury and was taken off on 90 as Wimbledon pumped long balls into our box. Not known for my heading prowess, I was the obvious man to make way.

My final game at home to Gillingham was the only time I started up front for Sheffield United in the three months I was there. I began well and flashed a left-footed shot just wide, then midway through the second half I cut in from the left and bent a shot towards the top corner but this time Vince Bartram pulled off a great one-handed save.

That was to be my last action as a Sheffield United player as I was subbed after the resulting corner. I had really enjoyed my loan spell, a lot more than I had done at Crewe, but my overriding emotion was one of disappointment because I was still to score a senior goal and that is what forwards are there to do and are judged on.

Scoring goals masks any average performance but if you're not finding the back of the net then as a forward there is no hiding place and deep down, I knew I hadn't done myself justice in either of my loan spells away from Liverpool, that I was a better player than I had shown either club.

The most frustrating thing, though, was that in the eight games I started in my loan spells only once did I play up front.

All I wanted was a chance and for a manager to play me in the position I knew I could succeed in. You could play any centre-forward wide and they would all do 'a job', but playing as centrally on the shoulder of the last defender was my biggest strength and it was never used at either Crewe or Sheffield United.

Once I was back at Liverpool, I became frustrated, as I would constantly find myself playing out wide rather than up front and that was hard, particularly when I felt I was a better player, and had shown that, than the players I was moved about for. My attitude, though, never changed, and I worked as hard as I always had done. But the fact that I was being moved here there and everywhere to accommodate other young strikers like Haukur Guðnason, Daniel Sjölund and even the transfer-listed Titi Camara, who had been told he had no future at the club, was a sign that the manager had made up his mind that my future lay elsewhere and I knew my time at the club was coming to an end.

Liverpool had sold Rigobert Song to West Ham and as part of the deal signed the young Finnish striker Sjölund, who was valued at £1m. He went straight into the reserve team up front against Newcastle and I was pushed out wide again up against Olivier Bernard, who would go on to play over 100 games in the Premier League for the north-east side.

I scored in a 1-1 draw and gave another good account of myself, but reserve games had become boring. Not in a sense that it was too easy, because it wasn't. You were playing against quality players, so it was always a test, but I'd loved playing first-team football with the game really meaning something to the players.

I wanted more of that and knew I wasn't going to get games at Liverpool, plus – being totally honest – I knew I was a little bit short of the quality and mentality that was needed to play in the Premier League week in week out.

Confidence is key to any footballer and when I was playing with confidence I knew I was good, but when my confidence was low, I could struggle.

Often the problem in games in which I played poorly was not my ability, even though fans or people outside the game would argue it was. It was about my confidence being so fragile that it affected my ability. You don't lose ability. You train for years perfecting your technique, but you do lose confidence. It is difficult for some people to understand, but it shows why the best players in the world don't just have the most ability – they also have the most mental strength.

It's a horrible feeling for a footballer who knows they are so much better but can't find a way back to the level they know they should be at.

People often ask me who was the best player I ever played with at Liverpool. There was so much quality it is almost impossible to answer, but the best always had confidence, an ego, even arrogance at times. Not arrogance in a bad way but arrogance that they were the best and that is absolutely key to being successful in sport in my opinion.

Three players who spring to mind for slightly different reasons are names I played with all the way through my early years, from youth level to the first-team squad – Steven Gerrard, Michael Owen and Jamie Carragher.

From an early age Steven was outstanding with his vision, passing ability and tackling. He was brilliant, but one thing he had more than any other player I've seen was a will to win. His drive to be the best individually and push his team on was unbelievable. His ability was on another level. His range of passing, his creativity, intelligence on the ball was as good as any of the world's greatest players throughout the years.

I've had so many arguments with people over the years who say Lampard or Scholes were better players. I never played with them and watching them they were great players and I know that I am biased, but Gerrard had everything. There was no weakness in his game. He was totally obsessed about being the best player he could be.

He has had great success as a manager already with Glasgow Rangers with other former Liverpool coaches Michael Beale and Tom Culshaw alongside him, which is no surprise having seen him work at Liverpool's academy. He is meticulous in his detail and organisation. He is creative, inventive and leaves no stone unturned to get the best out of the players he is working with and he has every chance of being as successful a manager as he was a player.

As a player he was without doubt the best I ever played with and when Liverpool found themselves in difficult periods over the years, he had the ability to drag them almost single-handedly through any bad times.

Michael Owen, as I have already alluded to, had a self-belief and self-confidence about scoring goals more than anyone I've seen. It was almost like 'if I want to score I will' and his pace gave him that edge. He was not just a goalscorer, he was more than that and went on to win the Ballon d'Or in 2001.

Carra was different in that people say, 'Oh he didn't have as much ability as some, but he just worked harder.' Yes, he did work hard but trust me, Carra had ability and for me was underrated. He wasn't as naturally gifted as Gerrard or Owen but he could play, and he absolutely loved the game. He was a leader, a great passer of the ball and was unbelievably brave as a defender. He would have played in his bare feet. Football was everything to him.

He absolutely hated losing, even in training, and if players let him down, even in a five-a-side game, they would get it off him no matter how good they thought they were. He was ultra-competitive, and his knowledge of the game was frightening.

All three of them, character-wise, were special. They had that inner mental strength which I didn't see from all the other younger players who were coming through at the same time, and I include myself in that.

Yes, they were brilliant footballers while we were good ones, but they also had the attitude that they were good enough to be there and they didn't care if they had to upset people to get where they wanted to be.

Football is a team game, but individually you must fight to get to the top. To play for Liverpool and be successful you have to tick every box.

Football does not wait for you. You have to make it happen yourself and those three in particular were not only great players, they had almost a 'fuck you' attitude and took control of their own destiny, making it impossible for them not to be Liverpool players.

Others were technically brilliant; Šmicer, Berger and Redknapp in particular fell into that category. Robbie Fowler was without doubt the best and most natural finisher I ever played and trained with. He was a massive help to the younger strikers, always talking to us and giving us tips, but because I saw so much of and played with Stevie, Carra and Michael a lot throughout our youth years and followed them into the first-team squad, I would say those three always stood out.

My final action for Liverpool was a reserve game at Villa Park. I had always enjoyed playing at Aston Villa. The pitch was massive and there was a lot of room to use my pace.

I had scored in the same fixture the previous year, a header off a Stig Bjørnebye corner – and if I was scoring headers off corners then it definitely was a lucky ground for me!

A couple of days earlier my agent had rung me to say that there were a few League One clubs wanting to take me on loan and a few of the managers would be at the Villa game.

I knew Bury were one of those clubs, as their manager Andy Preece had rung me to say he was desperate to sign me as his team were struggling and needed some pace up front.

I played well at Aston Villa. We won 4-2 and I scored once and was involved in everything that the team did well. After speaking on the phone while travelling home to my agent, who had also been at the game, I knew there would be no shortage of takers based on my night's work.

I was leaning heavily towards Bury as Preece had been adamant that he was signing me to play up front and the position I was going to play was going to be key to my decision as it would give me the chance to perform at my best.

The day after the Aston Villa game, there was only light training at Melwood with the first-team in the middle of a heavy schedule. Most of the players had already left when Gérard

Houllier and Phil Thompson asked to see me in the manager's office. They told me Bury and Wrexham wanted to take me on loan immediately and the choice was mine as to where I went.

'Both of them have got shite pitches,' was all Thommo said. I found out that was true very quickly.

The choice was left up to me as to where I went, but I think we all knew that I had probably kicked my last ball for Liverpool.

The first-team were progressing in three cup competitions – they would eventually win all three – and in the two months I had been back at Liverpool the club had signed Jari Litmanen from Barcelona, who at one stage in his career had been one of the best strikers in Europe.

He was past his peak when he arrived at Anfield, but some of the things he did in the three weeks I trained with him demonstrated the genius he was.

When you are down the pecking order anyway and then the club sign a player like Jari Litmanen I think it becomes obvious it is time to move on.

When I got back to the dressing room after speaking to the manager, Melwood was deserted so I threw my shin pads, running trainers and three pairs of boots into a black bin bag ready to take to my new club and left.

As I walked to the car, I took one last look at the training pitches which had been home to me for the last 12 years. I knew I wouldn't be back. I had been at Liverpool since I was nine years old and I loved the club, but I wasn't emotional about leaving. It was the right time, and I knew it.

It was only a loan spell but for some reason I knew my time at Liverpool was over. Even though I had only made four appearances for the first-team I had still done something that most people could only dream of, especially for a lifelong supporter.

The upbringing I had at the club was the best anyone could wish for. I had worked with three of the best youth coaches the country had ever seen and then trained with some unbelievably talented players. Liverpool Football Club would always be a part of me.

It is a unique club and city that has seen both triumph and tragedy. I wasn't born in Liverpool but because my dad and all his family were, because I've lived in and around the area for so long and spent so many years at the club, firstly as a supporter, then as a player and now as an academy coach, I see it as my home.

When you have been in and around it for as long as I had, Liverpool and what the club and the city represent becomes a part of you as a person. It becomes engrained in you and it never leaves you.

It had been a privilege to play for Liverpool but now it was time for a new start. I chose Bury and it felt right from the moment I made that decision. I could not wait to get started.

4

Different fuckin' class

BURY WERE an old club with a fantastic history. They had been FA Cup winners twice early in the 1900s and some football greats such as Terry McDermott, Neville Southall and the great Colin Bell had played for the Lancashire club.

However, that fantastic history seemed a long time ago and the club found it tough financially in the modern game.

Bury were living on the doorstep of more illustrious clubs in the north-west and were only getting gates of 3,000 or so, as many people who lived in the town supported either Manchester United or Manchester City, which frustrated their die-hard fans.

For me, Bury had been just one of the north-west clubs that my dad had taken me and my brother to occasionally when Liverpool weren't playing at home. Now it was to be my new club.

I drove up to Gigg Lane that same evening after leaving Melwood to meet the chairman Terry Robinson and watch Bury's game against Chesterfield in the cup.

I liked Terry straight away. He is a real down-to-earth fella with a dry sense of humour, and I had a great relationship with him while we were both at the club.

I watched from the directors' box with him as Bury went 3-0 down after just half an hour and some fans were already walking out.

Terry turned to me and said bluntly, 'You haven't signed yet, are you sure you don't want to fuck off and I'll tell the gaffer you changed your mind?'

I had to laugh and hoped things would only get better. They did, sort of. The second half finished goalless and Bury only lost 3-0.

Terry took me downstairs to meet the manager Andy Preece and his assistant Billy Ayre. They were furious about the performance and said the team needed pace and that they had both watched me play and that I could be just what the club needed.

The two of them came across well, showing a genuine interest in me, and knew a lot about me. They had done their homework and it was always good to feel wanted.

I had done my homework on the club as well and knew they were in the middle of a terrible run. They hadn't won in 14 games and had lost their previous four without a scoring a goal.

I was getting used to going on loan to different clubs and was finding going into new dressing rooms less daunting.

Bury was another world from Liverpool where everything had been done for us. Here it was the other way around, but things like that had never bothered me. I had never been a big-time Charlie. I had not done anything to be big time about.

As at Crewe and Sheffield United, there were some big characters in the Bury dressing room. Captain Nick Daws and his mate Chris Swailes were the experienced leaders with the Yorkshire car school of Paul Reid, Chris Billy, Paddy Kenny and Sam Collins trying to pull off a friendly coup and rule the roost.

I got on really well with Paddy and the Yorkshire lads and there was a really good team spirit despite results not being good. Ex-Manchester City centre-back – and Scouser – Steve Redmond was another big player.

Redo could play but he also had the no-nonsense defender tag down to a tee. A few times in games he would smash the ball into row Z as hard as he could, and when you looked at him with your arms outstretched as if to say keep it on the pitch he would turn and snarl at you, 'They can't score in the car park, kid.'

My debut for Bury was on 3 February 2001 at home to Peterborough United, but the day before I still had a few bits and bobs to sort out with the club secretary. I was waiting outside the manager's office at Gigg Lane after training when the office door almost came off its hinges as it smashed into the wall with an angry Sam Collins almost falling out of it, calling the manager every name under the sun.

It was a bit different to what I had been used to at Liverpool! We had done a bit of team shape that morning in preparation for Peterborough and Sam had not been in the starting XI and wasn't shy in letting Preecey know what he thought of the decision to leave him out. It was certainly an eye-opener for me on my first day.

I was really looking forward to the game and was playing up front alongside the manager. He was the type I liked playing alongside, similar in style to Erik Meijer, winning his headers and holding the ball up while I ran into the space off him.

The game got off to an electric start and I could have scored a hat-trick in the first ten minutes.

A long ball in the first minute dropped over the Peterborough back line and as the centre-half Simon Rea turned, I realised he couldn't move. He had about eight yards on me, but with my pace I got to the ball first and was in.

However, instead of just putting it past the keeper I tried to make sure I scored by going around him for a tap-in but the ball was blocked on the line.

Strangely enough, though, that miss gave me a massive confidence boost. The centre-half already knew he was in trouble with his lack of pace.

Five minutes later came chance number two as Preecey crossed from the left and I side-footed a volley off the bar.

On the outside I stayed calm but inside I was screaming that I had missed two chances to finally get off the mark.

The third chance came a couple of minutes later when I controlled a long pass from Paul Reid and hit a left-footed shot that was well saved by the keeper.

I didn't bother keeping my cool this time, screaming at the top of my voice and thinking I was destined to never score a first-team goal. There was a real buzz in the ground though. You could feel it. There were only about 2,700 fans there but they were getting right behind the team, sensing that my pace was going to give us a real threat all afternoon.

Peterborough somehow got to half-time with the game still 0-0, but other than lacking a goal, my debut had been excellent.

Preecey and Billy didn't mention the missed chances at half-time. They kept everything positive instead.

'Keep going. They're scared to death of you,' they kept emphasising.

I knew that I would get more chances and the next one came in the 56th minute. I laid a pass off to Reidy and spun in behind. Reidy just hit the space knowing I would get there. The keeper came flying out of his area and I slid in to win the 50-50 ball and as it broke loose on the edge of the box I managed to get there just before defender Andy Edwards and side-foot it towards the empty goal at the Manchester Road End at Gigg Lane.

Edwards made contact with my standing leg in what would have been a straight red card these days, but as I hit the floor, I heard the roar of the crowd as the ball hit the back of the net. Finally, my first senior goal – and ironically, I didn't even see it go in.

I was in agony on the corner of the box, my face buried in the Gigg Lane pitch, which was a mixture of sand and mud with not much grass. Phil Thompson was right.

I was helped to the side of the pitch by physio Alan Raw but a massive weight had been lifted from my shoulders with that goal.

The crowd gave me a great reception as I hobbled back on and for a team who had not won for so long the belief on the pitch and in the stands was evident.

We won 2-1 with our second goal coming from Sam Collins, who had come on in the first half, and him and Preecey celebrated together over by the corner flag by almost having a fight on the pitch instead of in the manager's office like the day before!

For me the debut couldn't have gone any better. My first senior goal, man of the match and a victory for the team.

As I left the pitch, Billy Ayre was stood at the entrance to the tunnel and said three words to me that made me feel ten feet tall. 'Different fuckin' class,' he said as he hugged me with a massive smile on his face.

The lads were absolutely buzzing in the dressing room after such a long wait for a win. It is amazing what one win can do to change the mood and direction of a football club. The message from the manager was 'push on from here' and over the next few weeks we did, as the following Saturday we went away to top-of-the-table Walsall and won 2-1 with goals from Nicky Daws and Steve Redmond.

It felt great to be an integral part of a team and having something real to fight for every weekend, which I knew I wouldn't get that at Liverpool.

The early weeks at Bury just clicked for me. Everything felt right, the place, the people at the club, the football on the pitch.

Billy Ayre was someone I hit it off with straight away as a coach, and he was my type of person. He was very down to earth and demanded certain standards. I think he saw similar in my personality. A piece written in the local press said as much, 'Bury coach Billy Ayre has revealed why he thinks Liverpool loan star Jon Newby has been such a success – because he's not stuck up!

'Ayre said that although Newby played for a Premier League club and was used to some of the best facilities in the country, he had not been afraid to roll up his sleeves at Gigg Lane and get stuck in.

"'The lad has been a delight since he came here from Liverpool," revealed Ayre. "There's no airs and graces about him. He's done everything we've asked of him in training and on a Saturday and he's come up trumps every time.'"

Another moment that stuck in my mind from my early days at Bury was a call I received from Sheffield United's assistant manager Kevin Blackwell in the days after I had scored against Peterborough.

I got on really well with Blackie and had confided in him how desperate I was to score my first goal. For him to ring and congratulate me that week meant an awful lot and I would always remember the gesture.

After the Walsall game, Bury signed forward Colin Cramb on loan. I had played with Cramby at Crewe and he was a great lad, a real character, the life and soul of any dressing room and we had a great relationship on and off the pitch.

Sometimes you don't know the reason why, but as a strike pair you just click and that was me and Cramby. He wasn't blessed with pace, but he could play. He was intelligent, creative, had a football brain and a real personality on the pitch as well as off it and the two of us loved playing together.

I remember us losing 4-1 at Reading. Cramby was sent off midway through the second half and gave the referee plenty of stick as a result.

After the game the ref's suit was found soaked in the shower, but nobody seemed to know how it ended up there – although Cramby didn't half find it funny when the official knocked on our dressing room door wringing his jacket out!

His debut, and our next home game, was against Oxford United. Our pitch, which resembled a beach due to rugby league team Swinton Lions sharing the ground for nearly ten years, was almost impossible to play any real football on, and although it wasn't Anfield I was really enjoying calling Gigg Lane my home.

I scored early in the game after controlling a pass from local lad Martyn Forrest to fire home and this time I was able to celebrate by heading to my mum, dad and brother, who had listened to my moaning for the last year about not scoring.

They had felt the frustrations as much as I had. We had too much for Oxford on the day and I grabbed my second goal with my left foot after great work by Paul Reid.

Reidy was an experienced midfielder at that level having played for Bradford City and Huddersfield Town and I loved playing in front of him. He had a great left foot, understood how we could hurt teams with me running in behind, and was a pleasure to play with.

We went on to win 3-1 and after no victories in 15, we had three victories on the bounce and were the form team in the league.

We travelled to Colchester later that week where I crossed for the manager to fire home a late equaliser, and we were unbeaten in four.

Another away point at Port Vale followed, where I made a goal for Cramby to open his account, and the run was extended to five games.

A few days later we faced the league leaders Millwall at Gigg Lane. They were the big spenders of the division and went on to win the title.

They had ex-Tottenham man Stuart Nethercott and the now Burnley manager Sean Dyche at centre-back, Lucas Neill at right-back and Neil Harris up front. Harris gave them a very early lead.

We had greater belief after recent results and Cramby equalised half an hour later with a superb individual goal, nutmegging Dyche in the process.

Millwall knew they were in a game and in the final minute of injury time Reidy floated a corner into the box and Sam Collins won a header which fell at my feet ten yards out, so I smashed it with the outside of my right foot into the top corner. Gigg Lane went wild, and we had surely sorted Preecey out with a manager of the month award thanks to that last-gasp winner.

In the six games since I had joined we had won four and drawn two, taking 14 points out of a possible 18. I'd scored four goals and made another two – it couldn't have gone any better.

My month's loan was almost over. Bury were desperate to keep me and I was desperate to stay. I felt at home. I spoke to my agent and he told me Liverpool were willing to let me leave permanently, as I had thought.

There were rumours that West Bromwich Albion in the Championship were interested, but there was nothing concrete and I didn't want to sign for a club and find myself a squad player. I was wanted at Bury where they saw me as the number one striker.

I loved it there and thought at that stage in my career, after two false starts away on loan, that it was the right move and club for me.

Bury were desperate to get the deal done as soon as possible and asked me what money I wanted in order to sign.

At Liverpool I was on a basic wage of just under £1,000 a week with signing-on fees and appearance money on top of that, but I almost doubled that at Bury and I would also get ten per cent of any transfer fee should they sell me on in the future.

Bury paid Liverpool £100,000 and the Reds were also due 50 per cent of any future profit on me, but I left that to the money men of the two clubs and was delighted to put pen to paper on a two-and-a-half-year deal.

I was happy to start a new chapter in my football career and I finally felt like I was a first-team footballer. Financially it was a great deal but from a football perspective it was even better and Bury was the only club that I wanted to sign for.

The *Liverpool Echo* reported on my departure by saying, 'It was farewell to Liverpool striker Jon Newby this week. Newby, who made a handful of substitute appearances for the Reds, signed for Bury in a deal which will increase in profit for Liverpool if the youngster goes on to bigger and better things.

'He's settled at Gigg Lane where manager Andy Preece has taken the novel approach of playing the striker in attack rather than as a winger. Dario Gradi and Neil Warnock take note!'

The deal was done, and I was officially a Bury player. I couldn't have been happier. The Bury website broke the news to the supporters later that night: 'We can confirm that current Liverpool loan star Jon Newby has signed for the Shakers on a long-term deal.

'Liverpool received three enquiries for the popular striker, all three from Premier League or First Division [as the Championship was then known] clubs and all involved cash deals. Liverpool did not receive any firm offers and offered 22-year-old Newby to Bury for an undisclosed fee.

'Shakers chairman Terry Robinson told the club website, "This is the deal of the season. We cannot thank Liverpool Football Club and Gérard Houllier enough. Talk of the big clubs helping out the little clubs being a non-event is thrown into the fire with this move. I am delighted that Jon has come to Bury and even more delighted that he wants to play for Bury."

'Manager Andy Preece was said tonight to be on cloud nine after hearing the news and said, 'We thought we would have to pay around three quarters of a million pounds for Jon, at least. As soon as I saw him, I said to the chairman that we had to sign him. If we can attract players of his quality to the club then we've got a chance.'

'Newby has been a revelation since arriving at Gigg Lane in early February. He has so far scored four goals and has only been on the losing side once.'

We were still hovering just above the relegation zone, despite the great run we had been on, and my first game as a permanent Bury player was away at Wrexham – the other club who had wanted to take me on loan. The first half was uneventful with no goals, but the game sprung to life on the hour mark when Wrexham's Dave Ridler was sent off for an elbow on me.

To be fair to him it was a total accident as we both jostled for the ball and as he lost his balance he fell backwards and his elbow smashed me in the eye. I went down holding my face.

The ref didn't hesitate and showed him a red card straight away and I proceeded to get booed by the Wrexham fans every time I touched the ball.

We eventually made our numerical advantage count in injury time when a perfect Colin Cramb through ball left me one-on-one with the keeper and I lifted it over him to confirm a vital three points that would go a long way to securing our status in the league that season.

As I scored, the momentum of my run took me round the back of the goal toward their Kop where I got showered with abuse and a few angry Welsh lads running down the terrace to tell me how much they had enjoyed watching me play that night!

I responded by smiling at them and putting my hand to my ear, referring to the fact I'd been booed for the last half an hour.

However, when I got back to the dressing room, I was told that I had to go and have a chat with the local police as there had been complaints that I had made a two-fingered gesture to the Wrexham faithful after I had scored.

The police basically laughed it off but for years afterwards I was public enemy number one with Wrexham supporters for something that genuinely never even happened.

As we headed towards the end of the season we were in good form as we beat Swansea City 3-0 at home, drew 1-1 away at Oldham Athletic, where I made a goal for Cramby, and on the Saturday that week and then travelled to Luton Town's Kenilworth Road.

There were still a few games left after that one but a win would guarantee our safety and keep us up. Just before we went out the manager gave us a further incentive to get the three points by saying, 'If we win, I don't want to see you until Thursday.'

There were a few things that motivated lower-league footballers, especially at that stage of a long season. Winning, the win bonus that followed, or days off. And not always in that order!

On the day Luton had the best player on the pitch by a mile in Matty Taylor, who went on to have a long Premier League career with the likes of West Ham and Portsmouth, and he gave them the lead.

As the game approached the final minutes with the score 1-1 an under-hit back-pass left Cramby clean through.

Every Bury player held their breath as he got closer to the goal. Our safety and four days off were riding on this finish. Cramby made no mistake and en masse we followed the scorer over to the dugout and jumped all over the manager, reminding him of his earlier statement.

He was true to his word and we got our days off. Most importantly, though, we had secured our status in the third tier of English football and, although we finished the season with a 3-1 defeat away at Brentford, the second half of the campaign had been a massive success for me.

I was 22 now and needed to be playing regular first-team football. I had the opportunity to do that at Bury with a manager and coach who believed in me and supporters who had really taken to me.

I had scored five goals since I had signed for Bury and even got a mention at the end-of-season Professional Footballers' Association awards bash in London regarding my performances. I couldn't wait for the new season to start.

5

The club have accepted a bid for you

WHEN THE new fixtures came out in the summer, we had a tough start and were away to Tranmere Rovers in the opening game then at home to QPR the week after.

There were a few changes in the close season. Cramby had signed for Fortuna Sittard in Holland and would be a big loss. We lost captain Nicky Daws and another leader in Chris Swailes. Our assistant manager Billy Ayre was missing too, as he had been ill over the summer and was temporarily replaced by youth team coach Andy Feeley. Andy was a very different character than Billy but a good coach and someone I liked.

Pre-season was very different compared to the Swiss mountains I had been to with Liverpool – instead it was the Welsh valleys of Carmarthen for a few days for us that year.

The week before the first game, Preecey called a meeting at the ground to announce that Billy wouldn't be coming back to the club for a while as he had been diagnosed with cancer. It was a massive shock to us all and a blow to me personally as I had such a good relationship with him.

The manager asked all the players to ring Billy that week to give him a boost and let him know that we were supporting him in his fight. How many of the other lads rang Billy I don't know, and I didn't do so just because the manager had told us to.

I called because he wasn't just my coach, he had become a friend and someone I had built up so much respect for in such a short space of time.

As I expected, Billy didn't want to talk about his situation. He wanted to ask how pre-season had gone and if I was ready for the Tranmere game. It was typical of him that he was concerned about the team rather than himself.

It later transpired that he had been diagnosed towards the end of the previous season but had been coming in to take training and then going to the hospital for his treatment in the afternoon. What a man.

Anyone who knew him would not be surprised by that, though. His enthusiasm for the game rubbed off on everyone and he was one of the main reasons why we had finished the previous season so well a few months earlier.

I was determined to get a goal for him in the opening game and the day before I made a T-shirt with a message showing my support for Billy. The day took on even more importance after speaking to him.

The T-shirt never happened as the writing was slightly visible under the kit and a busy linesman decided I had to take it off before the game. I came close to getting the quickest booking of the season in the tunnel after giving him a bit of stick. He only needed to let me wear it for the first three minutes as I scored the quickest goal of the 2001/02 Football League season.

In Italy you get a crate of 24 bottles of red wine for that. In England not a thing. I wasn't a drinker anyway so the goal would do nicely.

What a start to the season, a goal in our first attack and the lads bundled me into the back of the net in front of our large away following in celebration. The T-shirt would have been brilliant to show the supporters just how valued Billy was at the club by us all.

Tranmere levelled before half-time, but we always looked dangerous on the break and we got a late winner when Paul Reid fired home at the back post to get us off to the perfect start. We deserved to follow it up with another win the following week against QPR, but we hit the woodwork twice and lost 2-1 after playing really well again.

After the first two games there were signs of real promise about the season, but within the next five or six weeks it had totally unravelled, and we went on a horrendous run. Including the QPR game we lost eight in a row.

Over the bank holiday weekend we lost 2-0 at Huddersfield Town and 3-0 at home to Swindon Town, who were managed by my old Liverpool boss Roy Evans.

The next home match was against Stoke City and was the start of a crazy personal run for me during which I hit the crossbar or the post in five consecutive fixtures.

They say all strikers need a bit of luck and that was definitely the case for me at this time. Stoke beat us 1-0, then we lost 3-2 at Bournemouth and 1-0 at Port Vale before further defeats followed at Wigan, Oldham and Wrexham.

Wigan were miles better than us and beat us 2-0 without getting out of third gear.

Oldham was a strange game. We went 1-0 down in the first half but were still in it until substitute Gareth Seddon was sent off for dissent ten minutes after coming on. A quarter of an hour later we were 4-0 down and in disarray at the foot of the table.

If results were leaving the manager tearing his hair out, then an incident at Oldham wouldn't have helped. As we went 2-0 down I looked at the bench to see my number being held up. I was surprised in truth but reluctantly I jogged off the pitch. In those days the dugouts at Oldham's Boundary Park were about ten steps up in the stand and as I shook hands with the substitute and got a pat on the back from Andy Feeley, who had been holding my number up, I saw the manager come crashing down the steps, eyes bulging and shouting, 'Nooooooo! You've got the wrong number!'

He tried to push me back on the pitch, but it was too late, the change had been made and for the next 25 minutes Andy got dog's abuse off Preecey.

It was the last game Andy Feeley was involved in for the first-team. He eventually left after issues away from the game, but I am always of the attitude of taking people as you find them. Andy was always very good to me and was a very likeable fella who I always enjoy talking about the old days with when I occasionally see him now.

Preecey moved quickly to bring in more experience on the touchline and appointed Graham Barrow, who had been an experienced manager at that level, as his new assistant before our trip to top-of-the-table Reading. Before then, however, we had an away game at Wrexham where I was sure to get another interesting reception after the previous season's 'incident'.

We battered them but just could not score and going into the last 20 minutes a ball over the top put me clean through. Just as I was getting to the ball the centre-back grabbed my shirt and dragged me to the floor inside the box.

It was a clear penalty and a red card. The referee gave neither and totally bottled it. I could understand if we had been at Anfield in front of 45,000, but it was at Wrexham in front of fewer than 4,000 fans.

The centre-half knew he had got away with it and to make matters worse, I hit the post with less than five minutes left. Then, with the injustice of the penalty decision still on my mind, I lost my head as the final whistle blew.

I headed straight for the ref but got the silent treatment from him in response. Preecey was worse than me, understandably, as he was coming under real pressure from the fans with the run of results we were on.

The ref said something to the manager about it not being a penalty and the red mist descended on me as I told the referee exactly what I thought of him all the way up the tunnel.

As we got to his changing room, he told me he would be reporting me and I admittedly I tried to throw one last angry expletive his way before I got a sweaty goalkeeper glove over my mouth courtesy of Paddy Kenny who realised I was in enough trouble.

Once I'd calmed down, I couldn't even remember what I had said to the referee, but it capped off a miserable night and another defeat and would land me in trouble with the FA.

The game that finally ended the losing streak was Barrow's first with the club, at Reading's impressive Madejski Stadium – although at one stage it was looking like there wasn't going to be a match at all when the team coach broke down on the M6.

We were at the side of the motorway for an hour waiting for a replacement bus and a few Bury fans pulled up offering lifts. I didn't fancy a couple of hours cramped in the back of the old Ford Fiesta as good preparation, but one of the directors jumped in to make sure the club didn't get a fine due to the team sheet being handed in after 2pm.

The replacement coach that turned up, well, brown minibus, eventually got us to the ground half an hour before kick-off and by the time we were changed and had ten minutes to warm up.

Amazingly we started brilliantly, looking a threat every time we went forward and playing some great football on the carpet-like surface. I played a one-two with Reidy on the edge of the box and tried to pass the ball into the corner of the net but it came back off the post before rolling across the goal and the keeper smothered it.

I probably should have scored but surely, I was due a bit of luck. Despite only scoring once my performances had been consistently very good. I was creating chances and working the channels well and the only thing missing from my game was goals.

As I have said before, strikers are judged on goals scored and I wasn't scoring. Preecey and Graham were positive at half-time despite the fact we had gone a goal down just before the break.

We were still behind going into the last ten minutes and the manager had one roll of the dice left. I was about to get my fourth strike partner of the season after Baichung Bhutia, Gareth Seddon and the manager himself – and it was only September.

During the week, the club had re-signed Ian Lawson from Stockport County. He had been a fans' favourite at Bury a couple of seasons previously before being sold but he had been unlucky with injuries and was looking to kick-start his career again at Bury.

I took to the man known as 'Besty' straight away. His nickname was due to his similarities with the great George Best; not so much his playing skills but more his ability to sink a pint or three.

He was a hard-working player and a real down-to-earth lad who had an affinity for the club, and I wanted him to do well.

He made an immediate impact and slid in at the back post in the 93rd minute to equalise in front of the away supporters and we had finally got another point on the board – and at the league leaders of all places.

We celebrated by piling on Besty in the corner and I was delighted for him that he was back among the goals.

I also ended my own goal drought by getting my first since the opening day of the season in a 1-0 away win at a freezing Hartlepool United in the LDV Vans Trophy, with a right-footed volley in the 115th minute of a tie that went to extra time.

It was the first time I had scored a golden goal. The match was done and dusted, and it was nice to be back on the scoresheet. The night also saw the debut of left-back Jamie Stuart, who would go on to be an important player for us over the next couple of years.

It was an interesting week and one that I hadn't seen coming. I had phone calls from the manager and my agent, George Urqhart, within a minute or so of each other on the Thursday afternoon to tell me that the club had accepted a bid from Oldham Athletic for me.

George asked me if I was interested and said we should at least go and talk to them. Preecey, on the other hand, said he didn't want me to go and wasn't happy that the bid had been accepted.

It was in fact a joint offer of £450,000 for me and the up-and-coming left-back Chris Armstrong, who was an excellent young player. I was to be valued at a quarter of a million pounds and young 'Stretch' Armstrong at £200,000. I remember, however, that my first thought when I got the call was not one of excitement, it was, 'I don't want to go.'

I had only been at Bury for seven months and had fallen in love with the club. I had a great relationship with the manager who knew how to get the best out of me.

I had started every game since I had signed, I was playing in the position that got the best out of me, was on good money and had an unbelievable relationship with the supporters.

The Gigg Lane faithful sang my name at every game and they were not an easy bunch to please at the best of times so I must have been playing well. Why would I want to leave for a club in the same division taking all that into consideration?

Had it been a step up into the Championship then it would have had a great deal more appeal. I wasn't ruling a move to Oldham out totally, but I just didn't want to leave Bury.

I arrived at Gigg Lane early the following morning and met the manager who reiterated he didn't want me to go. Chairman Terry Robinson told me that although the club had accepted a bid due to financial reasons the decision was still mine.

It had been arranged that Chris and I would travel over to Oldham that morning to discuss the move. I sat in the dressing room feeling a bit flat. I had just made a new start and didn't really want to make another one so soon. By now a few of the lads were arriving for training and there was something in the paper about Luton Town preparing a bid for me.

Chris Billy waved his *Daily Star* at me. 'Luton, hey Newbs,' he said with a smile. 'Fancy it?'

'No, Oldham,' I replied.

'They in for you?' Ceebs asked.

'They've had a bid accepted. I'm going for talks this morning,' I said.

'Fuckin' hell, you're joking,' he said in shock.

I got on well with most of the lads at Bury and was well respected in the dressing room due to how well I'd done since I joined the club, and that was another reason why I was reluctant to leave. I had a final chat with the manager and headed over to Boundary Park where I would meet my agent.

I met Oldham's manager Andy Ritchie who came across well and spoke only about the football side of things. We didn't talk for long as he was taking training in preparation for their away game at Brighton the next day.

He said he hoped to see me at Brighton as Oldham's chairman wanted to fly both his new signings down to the south coast in his helicopter. My agent arrived and we then headed into a meeting with the club's chief executive about the terms of the contract they were offering.

His opening line before we had even sat down put me off straight away. 'You don't want to be a loser all your life, do you?' he said. 'Because you will be if you stay at Bury.' Fucking hell! He hadn't even said hello yet! My first thought when he said it was, 'Who the hell do you think you are?'

First impressions are key to me. It wasn't that I took it as a personal insult, I just didn't like the fact that he was having a go at my club, my manager and my team-mates and I told him that his opening line was hardly selling his own club to me.

He was there to promote his own club and belittling the team I played for should have been the last thing on his mind.

Oldham offered me a very similar deal to what I was already on, at just £100 a week more. If they had come in with a massive increase in my wages then I would have had to sit up and take notice but another £100 a week wasn't going to make any difference to whether I signed or not.

By the end of the weekend, after Oldham had lost 3-0 at Brighton, the offer had increased by another £100 a week but the money honestly wasn't a deal-breaker to me. I was also on ten per cent of the transfer fee so I stood to collect £25,000 from that too. With Liverpool on 50 per cent of the fee, Bury would have ended up with only £100,000 from the deal.

In order to get around that, the club were going to value Chris Armstrong at £445,000 and me at £5,000 so that there was no sell-on fee to pay, but out of that money Bury were still willing to give me the £25,000 I was due from the original agreed price.

It just shows how complicated transfers even at that level can be. I can't imagine what the biggest deals in football are like with agents owning players and all sorts of image rights.

I went through the formalities of completing a medical on the Friday and the CEO asked me if I had made a decision. I said I wanted the weekend to think about it.

He told me he didn't expect me to play for Bury the following day, but I told him while I was a Bury player I'd be playing if the manager wanted me to.

He was about as impressed with that as I'd been at his opening line. I went back to Gigg Lane for a chat with Preecey and told him I hadn't made a decision, but wanted to play the following day at home to Chesterfield in what was a massive game against one of our relegation rivals. That was good enough for him.

When I arrived at the ground the next day I think many fans were surprised to see me and, warming up I did feel mentally drained.

Knowing Oldham wanted me was a confidence booster. I had still only scored two goals that season so £250,000 was I suppose a gamble, but I knew how good my form had been since I had first gone to Bury in the February of that year.

The Bury fans gave me a fantastic reception but we found ourselves 1-0 down at half-time and the manager made a change, sending on Gareth Seddon to partner me up front for the second half.

He had an immediate impact and I raced down the left wing to whip a cross in for him to volley home at the near post. A couple of minutes later local midfielder Paul O'Shaughnessy slid a through ball to him and Seddon made it 2-1 with a great finish. The turnaround was complete and it was a big three points.

My relationship with Gareth was a strange one. He was a very good player and proved it away from Bury in later years. He was physical, athletic, quick and had an unbelievable strike on him and I loved playing alongside him. We both had a lot of energy and caused defences problems simply by not giving them a minute's peace, but off the pitch we didn't really speak. We were total opposites with Gaz a massive character in the dressing room whereas I was relatively quiet.

I started every game at that time, while he didn't, and I think that was part of the problem. Not all strike partners have to be best mates. We get on fine now when we see each other but the direct competition for a place in the team probably brought that situation out at the time.

That is the thing about football. Fans have this illusion that all the players are best mates, but at times they're not. Don't get me wrong, I've played in some teams where the team spirit has been brilliant, and everyone gets on, but everyone being best mates is not always healthy in team sport.

There has to be someone upsetting someone else to often get the best out of each other. I know from watching Liverpool in recent years that Luis Suárez and Daniel Sturridge weren't best mates – but look how good those two were together.

How many work colleagues in offices, factories and schools are best friends outside of work? Not many I would say. Yet at the same time I'd still give everything for my team-mates on the pitch, whether we got on or not.

I had, deep down, already made my decision to stay and told the manager after the game of that. I was turning down an extra £10,000 a year in wages and £25,000 as my share of a transfer fee so many people would say I was mad, but I did feel that by playing every week I could progress at Bury and if my form continued other clubs would be interested.

I also felt a sense of loyalty towards Bury and the manager, which I suppose is rare in football these days. I am certainly not trying to make myself out as some sort of crusader, but later down the line the club wouldn't show the same sort of loyalty towards me and neither would some of the supporters – but I suppose that's just football.

People have since asked me whether I regretted not signing for Oldham and I can honestly say that no, I didn't. That's nothing against Oldham as a club at all, I just felt that I was better suited to staying at Bury and Andy Ritchie was sacked three weeks later so who knows if the new manager would have fancied me as a player anyway.

Rumours about other clubs lining up bids for me continued after I had said no to Oldham and the chairman Terry Robinson told the local press, 'Jon is contracted to Bury Football Club and we hope he continues to play for Bury for as long as possible. Jon himself has recently stated that he is happy at the club and we see no reason to force him away from Gigg Lane.

'The financial difficulties widely reported in the media have been greatly alleviated by the sale of Chris Armstrong to Oldham, so the club is not about to sell its prized assets.

'We can confirm that Luton Town have been watching Jon but so have many other clubs. We have had no contact with Joe Kinnear or Luton Town, and we do not expect any.

'We wish to stop dead any rumour that Jon Newby is about to leave. He will remain a Bury player for the foreseeable future.'

We had two big games coming up after Chesterfield and next welcomed big-spending Cardiff City to Gigg Lane.

They had Spencer Prior, Danny Gabbidon and Rob Earnshaw in their team and were favourites to go up that year. They also had one of my former team-mates, Layton Maxwell, who, like me, had come through the youth system at Anfield for ten years.

I bumped into Maxi in the tunnel on the way out for the warm-up. 'You been playing well or something, Newbs?' he asked. 'Yeah all right, why?' I replied. 'Because our whole team talk was about you. Stop Newby you stop Bury,' he said.

Cardiff were managed by the experienced Lennie Lawrence and so it was nice to hear I was rated by someone like him.

On the night we were outstanding and were well worth our 3-0 victory. I made our final goal with a great through ball for David Borley for him to score the first senior goal of his career. Despite another good performance, though, I had missed a chance I really should have taken and knew I had to start adding to my goal tally.

The second of those games was at home to Bristol City, another of the top teams in the league. We had signed left-winger Harpal Singh on loan from Leeds United and he was a flying machine. With me and Gareth Seddon up front we had real pace and were a threat going forward.

We went a goal down early, but the game was very open, and we always looked likely to score. Despite my goal at Hartlepool in the LDV I still hadn't scored in the league since the opening day and it was now early November, which shows how well I had been playing despite not scoring to attract the bid from Oldham, as non-scoring strikers aren't normally in demand.

I finally got back on the scoresheet that night. Just before half-time there was a scramble in the box, and as I tried to head the ball goalwards I got a boot in the ribs from Bristol City left-back Matt Hill. The ref gave a penalty.

I was on the floor for about five minutes while physio Lee Nobes patched up my chest, but my first thought was that Reidy, our normal penalty taker, was suspended. As I sat up one of the lads asked me if I wanted to take it as there weren't many volunteers, so I was sat holding the ball for the last two minutes that I was on the floor.

Throughout my career I was always pleased that I never shirked responsibilities like taking penalties. I would rather miss than not offer to take a penalty. This was one penalty I couldn't afford to miss.

If I had, it may have had a negative impact on my confidence and made me wonder where the next league goal was coming from, but I took it confidently to the goalkeeper's left, sending him the wrong way, and I nearly ended up in Gigg Lane's South Stand with most of my team-mates on my back.

We carried our momentum into the second and Singh scored to give us what looked like another massive three points, but we had a bad habit of not being able to see games out and when a defensive header to Paddy Kenny fell short, Bristol City grabbed a last-minute equaliser and we had to settle for a point in a 2-2 draw.

The following day, I and Preecey had to travel to Birmingham as we had both been charged with misconduct by the FA for the incident in the tunnel at Wrexham. Having spoken to our PFA representative Mick McGuire, we both expected to get a fine. The one thing I didn't want was to get a ban and miss games.

I had accepted the charge knowing I was in the wrong, but still maintained it wouldn't have happened in the first place if the referee had got the decision right and given a penalty. The charge sheet against both of us was damning, but Preecey's list of crimes was without doubt longer than mine.

However, instead of a fine I was given a one-game ban with immediate effect, ruling me out of our next match on the Saturday against relegation rivals Colchester United. If the FA had heard what me and the manager were calling the three elderly men that made up the misconduct panel outside the room after the verdict, I think we would have both been given another charge.

I had no problem with being fined and wasn't expecting the club to pay it either; that would come out of my pocket. Most players would have just accepted the ban to save losing money and some of the lads thought I was mad, but I didn't want to miss games. We appealed straight away, which meant the whole process was halted until there was a second hearing, leaving me free to play at Layer Road. It proved to be a great decision as I scored an 88th-minute winner in a backs-to-the-wall 1-0 victory in which Kenny was magnificent in goal.

He had denied Colchester all afternoon and his growing reputation meant that he would deservedly be moving on to bigger and better things in the summer.

Michael Nelson also put in a superb performance at centre-back that day, having been brought in from non-league Bishop Auckland a few months earlier, and he would become a mainstay in the back four over the next couple of seasons.

The goal that won the game at Colchester was one of the best of my career, picking the ball up on the left and cutting inside past three defenders before firing home from just inside the box.

It had been a good week. We had got four points out of six and I had scored twice, despite my brush with the disciplinarians at the FA.

But if that was a good week then the following week was an absolute nightmare.

We had an FA Cup replay against Lincoln City from the division below after drawing 1-1 at Sincil Bank, conceding yet another equaliser in a game I should never have played in after dropping out of training on the Thursday with a slight pull in my thigh – but as I've said, if I could sprint then I would play.

In hindsight I wish it had been the replay I hadn't been fit for as I missed not one but two penalties and we crashed out of the cup. The game finished 1-1 and my first miss came in the first period of extra time when the keeper saved to his left. The second came in the shoot-out and this time it was a poor penalty as I switched sides but it was an easy height for the keeper to push it away.

As Lincoln scored the winning penalty, I slumped off to the dressing room disgusted with myself and got the usual 'don't worry, anyone can miss a pen' pats on the back off the lads, but it was an awful end to the night – and it just happened to be my birthday too.

The missed penalties fortunately didn't affect me too much and I was still in good form as the manager surprised me a couple of weeks later before our away game at Notts County.

He told me that with Paul Reid injured he was making me captain. It was something I hadn't expected at all. He explained that although I wasn't a typical captain in that I wasn't someone who would be shouting on the pitch, I led by example in my play, especially my work rate.

It may not seem much to some to be named captain of League 1 Bury, but to me it was everything and it was a very proud moment to lead the team out for the first time.

We won 2-1 and I really enjoyed my new role and the extra responsibility that went with it. I captained the side a few more times that season.

My FA misconduct charge also got put to bed as on my appeal my one-game ban was changed to a £300 fine. That was okay by me as I wanted to play in every game and try and help the club avoid relegation.

It was time to stop getting fined as well. I moan off the pitch anyway, but, on the pitch, it often helped me in terms of wanting to win. However, it was costing me a bloody fortune! I picked up three yellow cards for dissent. Our club rules meant that a first for dissent was a ten per cent cut from my weekly wage, the second 20 per cent and the third half a week's wage. With the FA cost added to those I lost a week's wage that season and I could have done without that.

Just before Christmas we played Blackpool at home in a game that finished 1-1 that should never have been played. A third of the pitch was frozen, where the South Stand roof didn't let the sun get to the pitch. It was like an ice rink. The decision to play was crazy.

I gave another good performance and there were rumours before the game that the Blackpool manager Steve McMahon was going to make a bid to take me to Bloomfield Road. Both myself and McMahon were interviewed by the press afterwards to ask if there was any truth in the story. I told them I didn't know anything about it, which was true, and McMahon said that he liked me and would be interested in signing me.

I took it as a massive compliment that a former Liverpool great, someone who had achieved so much in the game and someone that I had watched from the Kop many times, was interested in signing me.

I remember watching him score in front of the Kop in his final game for Liverpool, as we beat Nottingham Forest 2-0, and being disappointed that he would be leaving Anfield to join Manchester City.

The situation with Blackpool moved on somewhat after our next game, at Swindon Town. We lost 3-1 and were poor but I at least got on the scoresheet in the first half.

It was just into the new year that Blackpool made an official bid of £200,000 for me. Bury rejected it, telling my agent that it wasn't enough money due to the sell-on agreement with Liverpool and the ten per cent I was due. Blackpool upped their bid to £220,000, which was again rejected with Bury holding out for the £250,000 that Oldham Athletic had offered earlier in the season.

Again, I didn't try and force a move as I had no real desire to leave but I certainly would have listened to a club with the history of Blackpool and a manager like McMahon. We were due to play Blackpool away the following week and during the week McMahon was interviewed and asked if there would be any further bids for me. He told the press that 'any deal was dead in the water as I had said I was not interested and lacked ambition'.

It was disappointing to hear that as I had never said I wasn't interested, and I certainly didn't lack ambition. Blackpool were simply 30 grand short of what Bury were prepared to accept. We beat Blackpool and I set Gareth Seddon up for a tap-in for the only goal. However, McMahon was right in that the deal was dead and Blackpool never returned with a higher bid.

The week after Blackpool we faced high-flying Reading at Gigg Lane, when I scored the favourite goal of my career in a 1-1 draw.

Sam Collins played a great diagonal pass over the right-back's head and while on the run I controlled the ball in the air and slid it past the keeper. My first touch made the goal special.

We had been playing a slightly different system since Christmas with three in midfield, which helped us be more secure defensively but limited us a little bit going forward.

I was playing on the right or left of the forward three and was happy to do a job that helped the team, but I felt playing wide restricted my freedom to run the channels where I was so effective. I had to do far more defensive work, tracking a full-back, but as long as we continued to pick up points I was happy to play wherever I was asked to.

We had done well to give ourselves a chance of staying in the division after losing nine of our opening ten matches, and since Christmas had hovered just above or were just in the relegation zone.

We drew too many games we were in good positions to win, conceding a last-gasp equaliser at home to Oldham, drawing 2-2 with Wrexham and 0-0 with Huddersfield, and after being ahead twice against relegation rivals Cambridge United we conceded within two minutes both times.

We beat Bournemouth at home in a crucial game, with Ian Lawson and former Manchester United youngster George Clegg scoring our goals.

We then drew 1-1 at home to Port Vale, throwing away another two points late on.

I played wide right with the manager playing himself up front as, due to the state of the pitch, we had to play more direct.

I capitalised on a weak back-header to round the keeper and give us the lead with 20 minutes left, but even with Port Vale down to ten men we couldn't see the game out and results like that would ultimately come back to haunt us.

In a controversial defeat at Chesterfield we equalised with a couple of minutes to go, but as we celebrated a linesman wrongly ruled out the goal for offside as we later saw on the match video. While we celebrated, Chesterfield took a quick free kick and broke down the field to score again and seal victory. The door of the away dressing room at Saltergate took the brunt of the manager's bad mood and was smashed off its hinges as he walked in.

We lost 2-0 away at Bristol City, conceding two in the final ten minutes, and I again hit the post with the score 0-0.

We then gave ourselves hope of escaping the drop with a 2-0 win at home to Brentford with two superb Chris Billy strikes, but results went against us and with a poor goal difference we went into our final home game of the season against Colchester United needing a win or we were relegated to League 2.

We started it well and I was back up front in a two where I was much more comfortable and created two great chances for my strike partner that day, Ian Lawson. Besty was denied twice with the keeper making one superb save in particular, but those chances were as good as it got and despite a late Chris Billy consolation goal, we lost 3-1 and were relegated.

Even though it had been coming I was stunned. I had given absolutely everything to the cause, as did many of the lads, but I was physically and mentally shattered having started all 51 games, I'd only been subbed twice.

I couldn't have had a better season in terms of my performances, but I could and should have scored more goals. That was my one regret of the season. I had no regrets about not joining Oldham or not trying to push through the move to Blackpool, I just felt regret in that I hadn't scored enough goals for the team.

I was devastated about going down. I didn't speak to anyone for days and wouldn't leave the house because of a sense of embarrassment. No footballer wants a relegation on their CV, and I understood why. It was horrible.

We still had a meaningless game to play away at Peterborough the following weekend, so we were in for training that week and I found it difficult going into the club.

In my opinion we had let the supporters down. I don't know if any of the other players felt the same, but I had been a football fan long before I was a player. I would travel all over the country watching Liverpool at places like Crystal Palace, Wimbledon and Southampton and I often felt let down as a fan when the players didn't perform. I had no problem with any Bury fans giving us stick for the way that season ended, and I didn't expect to be exempt from any criticism.

On the Wednesday before the final match of the season we had the day off, but Preecey rang me just after 7am and I could tell straight away that something was badly wrong. And it was far more important than football; he told me that Billy Ayre had died.

It was a massive shock. Whenever I had spoken to Billy during the season, he always turned the conversation away from himself and on to football.

'Don't worry about me, son, I'll be fine. How are you playing?' he used to say.

The conversation with the manager that morning was so difficult with us both in tears. Preecey said, 'He thought the world of you,' before hanging up, too devastated to speak.

It was a desperately sad end to the season.

Football is often a strange industry where people come and go all the time, but it is not often you meet someone like Billy. I only worked with him for four months and in that time, I learnt so much from him. He became a mentor and a friend as well as my coach and when I think back to that first season, I can see still hear him say those three words to me as I walked into the dressing room after playing well; 'Different fuckin' class.'

They made me feel on top of the world and he knew that. He was taken from us far too early and his funeral at Halsall Church was standing room only. He was someone I will never forget.

The season finished with a 2-1 defeat at Peterborough, and I think everyone was glad when the final whistle blew. No result that day would have changed the fact that we were already down, and I just wanted the season to be over. We had a presentation night at the club a few days later and they are never easy when the season hasn't gone well, but I was pleased to win four awards – including supporters', manager's and players' player of the season.

The players' player is always the one you want to win as it shows a respect from your team-mates. I voted for Paddy Kenny who, although I didn't know it then, had played his last game for the club as he was sold over the summer for a ridiculously low fee of around £45,000 according to the press.

He had been immense all season and would go on to have a fantastic career in the Premier League. I was delighted for him.

The campaign, though, had ended in the worst possible way on the pitch and my stats with Bury stood at 68 games played and 12 goals scored. That could improve and I was determined it would in 2002/03.

6

If we don't get promoted, I will have to leave

ANDY PREECE was determined that we would bounce straight back into League 1 and pre-season was a tough shift that year, as we spent a lot of time at Tandle Hill Country Park near Oldham. I was a sprinter, so the long-distance slogs were never my thing, especially uphill.

We played two pre-season friendlies behind closed doors that year away from the supporters.

Firstly, we faced Blackburn at their training ground, and they had a mixture of first-team players and young pros. We were 3-0 up at half-time, with me scoring one and making another and I was feeling sharp after a rest in the summer.

However, the difference between our first- and second-half performances was that between chalk and cheese and the game finished 3-3. It showed the same problems that had seen us relegated a few months earlier, with us not being able to see matches out – and because of that the manager was fuming. He went mental in the dressing room and when he blew his top, you knew about it.

I had a few heated exchanges with him during our time together at Bury, but it was only because we were both so desperate to do well and I have to admit that the fact I was a moaning sod didn't help.

The way I saw it at times is that we were mates as well and when he had a go at me from the touchline during a game, I would have a go back at him if I thought he was wrong – as you do with mates. But he was my manager first and a mate second and I couldn't do that. He spoke to me in his office and said, 'I'm not fuckin' having it, Newbs.' He was right, and I apologised.

He was a manager I liked and respected more than any other I ever worked with as he knew how to get the best out of me. Although our disagreements weren't frequent, they were usually entertaining, but I would have run through brick walls for him with Bury.

At this Blackburn game, though, it wasn't us arguing with each other as he rounded on a few of the players he thought had under-performed the season before and laid into them. After about five minutes of going mad he turned, pointed at me and shouted, 'You're not fuckin' leaving everything to him again!'

On the one hand I was thinking at least he appreciated how much I put into last season and how well I did. On the other I was thinking, 'The lads are going to be all over me for this.' And there were a few teacher's pet shouts when Preecey eventually slammed the door and walked out.

The second game was a hastily arranged friendly at Blackpool, who were still in the league above us. Both teams were playing almost full-strength line-ups, with the season starting a few days later. I had felt really sharp in the games so far and that day was no exception.

We ripped Blackpool apart and I made a goal for Preecey and scored a good solo goal of my own as we won 2-0. Blackpool were still managed by Steve McMahon, who had wanted to sign me a few months earlier.

I remember coming off the pitch with about ten minutes to go and Chris Billy jokingly telling me it had been nice playing with me as Blackpool would be straight in for me after the match, but nothing ever materialised and I think that ship had definitely sailed – although it was nice to give them a reminder of what I could do.

There were also rumours in the press of Hull City, who were managed by Jan Mølby, preparing a bid for me at this time and I knew from speaking to Billy Ayre that he had earlier told the former Liverpool great, with whom he was close friends, to sign me should he ever get the chance.

The league season started a few days later and we lost 2-1 away at Oxford United. We didn't start playing until we were two goals behind and even though George Clegg got one back, we couldn't rescue a point.

I had a new strike partner that day and for the next few months, as we had signed Pawel Abbott on loan from Preston North End.

Pav was a really talented player and we formed a great partnership, especially in the opening ten games or so. He was big and strong and a good hold-up player, but he was also creative and could score goals.

He played with an air of confidence and arrogance and wasn't afraid to try things out of the ordinary. He knew he had ability and he backed himself. I wish that self-confidence had been something I had more of throughout my career.

Our first home game of the season was a couple of days later against Cambridge United, who were also looking to bounce back up after relegation, but we were beaten 1-0. The only place we were bouncing was towards the foot of the table.

Our next game was at home to Swansea City, and I got my first goal of the season by firing home from a low cross to put us 2-0 up.

It was so important to get off the mark and I felt relief rather than joy. We let our lead slip, though, and Swansea were level with 20 minutes to go, but I had a shot blocked on the line and centre-half Danny Swailes smashed the rebound home from close range to give us our first three points of the season.

Next up was a crazy game at home to Shrewsbury. For an hour we were like Brazil and for the last half an hour we were like, well, Bury!

Cleggy had an early penalty saved but I tapped in from all of six inches to give us the lead. My mate Lee Unsworth tried to claim the goal, but like any striker I was having none of it – even though it probably was over the line. Sorry, Unsy.

Our other loan signing, Terry Dunfield, a young Canadian from Manchester City, scored our second goal minutes into the second half and we were looking good for three more points.

Terry was as mad as a hatter, a real character and brilliant for team spirit. His quality on the pitch was evident as well and he was a superb signing for us with his personality being just what the dressing room needed having lost a couple of players that summer.

Terry's goal was added to moments later when I crossed for Pav to score his first goal for the club, and he returned the compliment crossing for me to half-volley the ball home with my left foot past my old Liverpool team-mate Ian Dunbavin to put us 4-0 up – and then it all nearly unravelled.

Experienced Shrewsbury striker Nigel Jemson scored a hat-trick in seven minutes and with Jemson being a former Bury player, plus a mate of Preecey's, that just made things even worse. We hung on, just, to win 4-3, but we had to improve on seeing games out.

I scored in the next game, away at Boston United, only for us to concede a 93rd-minute equaliser by not defending a long ball well enough. There were a few angry players in the dressing room as Preecey and Jamie Stuart nearly came to blows. How many times could we continue to throw points away?

My scoring run continued as I netted our first in a 2-1 win at home to York City. Pav added our second; our partnership was really coming to life as we climbed the table.

We then had a break from the league as we faced Championship side Stoke City in the League Cup at Gigg Lane. It was a game we could go into with no pressure on us and just enjoy.

We played one up front with me out wide on the right and tried to frustrate them and hit them on the break. We got the only goal of the game in the second half when I got isolated with one of Stoke's big centre-halves out on the right touchline and nutmegged him before standing a cross up to the back post for Jamie Stuart to head home.

Jamie was a very popular member of the team and despite only initially signing for us on a short-term deal, he stayed for two seasons. I was delighted for him to get the winner in a big game. Beating a side from two divisions higher was a great result and sent us into our next game at Bournemouth full of confidence.

Our mood there was further boosted by the news shortly before the game that we had been drawn away at local rivals Bolton Wanderers, then of the Premier League, as a reward for beating Stoke. The dressing room was buzzing before we went out and beat the best footballing side in the division that season with a Martyn Forrest penalty and a Lee Unsworth header giving us the three points.

As a team we were a close-knit group with a strong spirit, which without doubt helped us at times that season.

Every club I've been at, there has always been a song that's reminded me of the season. The trip to Bournemouth provided it for that campaign. In those days there was no Bluetooth-syncing your phone to the speakers, it was the old-fashioned ghetto blaster, and if the kit man hadn't packed it in for an away game it would be like he had forgotten to pack the kit!

We used the same CD for every game but when we pressed play that day the stereo was empty and the only music that we could find was a CD free in that morning's *Daily Star* of classic Disney theme tunes – so we had 'Under the Sea' from *The Little Mermaid* blasting out of thc away dressing room.

We won, so that was it for the season and the same CD stayed in. By Christmas we all knew every word to songs from *The Little Mermaid* and *The Jungle Book*!

With the Disney classics spurring us on we put in two more good performances, but only took a point in each game.

The first was a 1-1 draw at home to Hartlepool United. We then travelled to Wrexham, where I was again booed with every touch. Despite the crowd reaction Wrexham had always proved to be a lucky ground for me throughout my career and I scored a few goals there.

This time, though, it didn't look like I would even get a chance never mind a goal as we found ourselves two down and struggling to get out of our own half with Andy Morrell scoring twice.

The game changed with a red card as Wrexham's Carlos Edwards was sent off for an off-the-ball incident involving our new signing Colin Woodthorpe. Woody did me a big favour as he ended up getting more stick than me off the crowd for the rest of the game.

We capitalised on being a man up almost immediately, with Pav going on a mazy run down the left to pull it back for me to pass it into the corner of the net, and the comeback was complete midway through the second half when I intercepted a poor back pass to round Wrexham keeper Andy Dibble and smash it past the defender on the line.

I had a chance to win it and get my first senior hat-trick but Dibble denied me when I probably should have scored, and although we were disappointed with only a point after such a good performance it gave us plenty of confidence and set us up nicely for the cup game at Bolton.

Leading up to that tie I had been the skipper for a few games when club captain Martyn Forrest hadn't been in the starting line-up.

Foz was a local lad; his dad John was on the staff and had been a legendary goalkeeper for the club several years before. They were both Bury through and through but Preecey made the call to leave him out of the team to face Bolton after he reacted to being taken off at Wrexham. I was given the armband for what he said was the foreseeable future, but I felt for Foz as we all wanted to play at Bolton, not least a lad from Bury who knew all about the rivalry.

Walking into the Reebok Stadium was impressive. The pitch was being watered as we got there and looked immaculate. We were all set to take a big away following of about 3,500, with it being a local derby, and it looked set to be a great atmosphere. The only disappointment was that it wasn't a televised game. It was a Premier League against a team doing well in League 2 and there was the opportunity for a shock.

I was full of confidence having scored twice at Wrexham and I got a further boost when I ran out to warm up. I didn't like going out too early before a game and hated the two hours before kick-off with the nerves and the waiting around. I just wanted to get on with the game.

I used to leave going out on to the pitch until the very last second. Other lads would be out 45 or 50 minutes before kick-off but as long as you were out to start the team warm-up with 35 minutes to go then the manager was fine with that.

Chris Billy and I would always go out at the very last second every game. I had my usual ways, but Ceebs just hated the cold in the winter months!

That night, as we ran out towards a full away end, the whole stand started to sing my name, which was amazing to hear in a big ground in such a big game and atmosphere. It gave me a real boost.

Bolton fielded a weakened team but they still had Premier League quality in their line-up, which included former Real Madrid player and Champions League winner Iván Campo at centre-half.

I knew it was important to start well against a player with Campo's experience and quality, so the first thing I did had to be done well as I knew he wouldn't fancy chasing some busy centre-forward from three divisions lower around the pitch all night. After playing at the Camp Nou against Barcelona for Real

Madrid, he wouldn't be unsettled by a few thousand Bury fans giving him a bit of stick either.

It was again a proud moment to lead the team out as captain and we started really well when Pav sent me away down the left where I found myself one v one against Campo straight away.

I knocked the ball past him and ran. I knew he was a player with unbelievable quality, but I wasn't sure he was the most mobile and my pace took me past him. I pulled it back for Cleggy who tested the keeper in our first attack.

I knew straight away that I had Campo. That was how much of a confidence player I was. If the first thing I did in a game was good I knew I'd go on to play well, whereas if Campo had brushed me off when I tried to run past him that night it could well have gone the other way and I could have been anonymous.

To a man we were outstanding and we fully deserved to go ahead early in the second half. Pav put me away down the right and I sprinted into the box and slid a ball across the face of the goal, begging to be tapped home. Colin Woodthorpe and Bolton defender Bernard Mendy slid in at the back post and the ball ended up in the back of the net in front of the Bury fans. We were 1-0 up.

This time we didn't concede and neither did we just hang on. Our back three of Michael Nelson, Matt Barrass and Danny Swailes were superb and we had chances to extend our lead, but the one goal was enough and it was an amazing night, not just for us as players but also for the supporters who had seen us beat our local rivals again. To captain the team to victory against a Premier League side who had been Bury's fiercest rivals throughout their history was very special and one of the best nights of my career.

Our game on the Saturday was typically 'after the Lord Mayor's show' following that big win and we came back down to earth with a bump by losing 3-1 at home to Southend United – despite taking an early lead through Nelson.

We then picked up ten points from a possible 12 as we came back from 2-0 down at home to Darlington to draw 2-2, scoring twice in the last five minutes. We won 1-0 at Rushden & Diamonds, 2-1 at home to Macclesfield Town and 2-1 away at Leyton Orient where I set up the winner for Terry Dunfield to tap home.

Preecey wasn't going to play me at Orient as my grandma had died days earlier and I was struggling with that, but I convinced him to pick me and although I didn't have the best of games I did contribute with the assist for the winner.

Despite making goals, I hadn't scored for a while and our next game was away at Fulham in the next round of the League Cup.

We were disappointed with the draw as although Fulham were in the Premier League, they weren't a Liverpool or a Manchester United and weren't even playing at their own ground then – instead sharing with QPR at their Loftus Road stadium.

They were managed by Frenchman Jean Tigana and his philosophy was pass pass pass. That's just what they did. They must have had at least 75 per cent possession that night and we couldn't get near them. We were no match for them on a disappointing night and lost 3-1, a result made worse by losing influential midfielder Dunfield to a dislocated shoulder which would rule him out for a few weeks.

I grabbed a consolation goal in the last seconds after nicking the ball off a defender before running through to finish with my left foot. It was nice to get on the scoresheet against a Premier League team.

It was a unique game in that it was the first time that an English team had fielded a starting line-up made up of 11 different nationalities. How's that for a bit of boring football trivia?

We were a bit inconsistent after that, but were still very much in the race to get promoted. We lost at home to Torquay United and then won away at Carlisle United through a late Lee Unsworth header.

We then beat another team from a higher division, defeating Tranmere Rovers in the LDV Vans Trophy as I scored the first and made the second for a young David Nugent.

I got another goal in the home derby against Rochdale when we went 1-0 up but conceded late on when an offside trap that we had worked on went wrong and Unsy played Lee McEvilly on by about five yards for him to secure a point for Rochdale. This led to a full-scale brawl in our dressing room about whose fault the equaliser was!

We dropped more points over Christmas, losing 4-1 to Shrewsbury at a half-waterlogged Gay Meadow where we were awful, and then drawing 1-1 at home to Kidderminster Harriers. I scored a good goal in the game but hit the top of the bar late on when really, I should have scored, and the fans were just starting to get frustrated and giving me a bit of stick for missing chances.

There was talk at this time about Wigan Athletic, in the division above, being interested in me. Their manager was Paul Jewell, who my agent knew well, and he wanted to sign me as he thought I would help Wigan gain promotion from League 1 into the Championship.

It would have been a move that really appealed to me at that stage of my career as I would have been stepping up to a club that were very ambitious about getting to the Premier League, while not having the upheaval of relocating from the north-west.

My agent told me that Wigan were going to bid in the region of £40,000. The figure was so low because it was now almost February and I would be out of contract in four months.

Terry Robinson was no longer chairman and when Wigan made the enquiry his replacement told them I wasn't for sale at all as Bury felt they stood a better chance of getting promotion with me at the club.

I understood the reasons why the enquiry was turned down as £40,000 was neither here nor there with the ongoing financial problems at Gigg Lane, but I honestly think that if Terry had still been at the club he would have seen how much effort I had put in over those last two years and said, 'It's a chance to progress, if you want to go then you can.'

The move showed no signs of happening, though, and my agent told me they wouldn't be back as they turned their sights elsewhere; they went on to pay big money for Nathan Ellington, who was a massive success for them.

There was no sulking from me, but that is the one time that I think I would have moved from Bury, so that I could further my career. However, I was still desperate for us to get promotion.

It was no coincidence that as we were going through a rocky spell in terms of results we had lost Pav, whose loan from Preston had come to an end. This meant a change in system from 3-5-2 back to 4-3-3, with me playing out wide again. The manager moved to rectify it and brought Colin Cramb back on loan from Holland.

Preecey also brought in his long-time friend Andy Morrison, or 'Jock', as he was known. He was a Scotsman with the broadest West Country accent you'd ever heard, was at the end of his playing career and would be coaching the reserve team at the club. Jock was an absolute man-mountain, and he could still play. If he told you he was going to a ping a 60-yard pass to the big toe of your right foot he would do it, first attempt.

Jock and Cramby arrived the day before we played at Carlisle United in the LDV Vans Trophy and they both travelled with us to the game. This competition always starts off as a bit of a nuisance, especially to managers and players who don't want the extra fixture full stop, and to fans who don't want added expense.

As you progress through the rounds it becomes massive, as Wembley gets closer, and it may be the only chance for a lower-league player to appear at such a stadium, although at this time the finals were being played at Cardiff's Millennium Stadium while Wembley was being redeveloped.

There was already a bit of needle between the two clubs after our win at Brunton Park earlier in the season, in an ill-tempered game, and this was no different.

After trailing 1-0 at half-time, two stunning volleys from George Clegg and Terry Dunfield gave us a 2-1 lead. The tackles were flying in and Carlisle levelled in the last minute despite a push on Steve Redmond at the back post, so the tie went into extra time with the golden goal rule in play.

Carlisle had a centre-forward at the time called Richie Foran, who was actually a very good player but he could have started a fight in an empty house as he spent most of the night trying to scrap rather than play football.

People spoke about Billy Whitehurst and Duncan Ferguson being old fashioned centre-forwards. This lad could have given them a run for their money. Chris Billy eventually lost his cool and jumped in to a two-footed tackle on Foran right in front of the dugout which earned Ceebs a red card and saw a bust-up between the two sets of staff.

Just three minutes before a penalty shoot-out would have decided a winner, Carlisle scored with the aid of a massive deflection which wrong-footed our keeper Glyn Garner.

We were out. The Carlisle players and staff were running all over the pitch and we were devastated, as the dream of reaching the final was over.

I trudged over to our supporters to clap them for making the journey on a freezing night and Graham Barrow, our assistant manager, and I were the last two people walking down a very noisy and jubilant tunnel.

The tunnel at Brunton Park is quite long with a few twists and turns and as I made my way back to our dressing room, Foran, who was in front of me, turned and pressed his head against mine, taunting me about the result.

The rest of my team-mates by now were back in the dressing room and as we got alongside the door of Carlisle's dressing room,

Foran gave me one last mouthful of abuse and I gave him an old-fashioned rugby hand off to the face and shoved him. There was nothing in it but we both had studs on and on the slippery stone floor the pair of us went flying.

As we hit the deck the noise of us falling made the Carlisle players burst out of their dressing room, and as I got back to my feet me and Graham quickly realised that we were in no man's land with the whole Carlisle squad ready to go to war.

I then heard our dressing room door fly open behind me and our lads, with new boys Jock and Cramby at the front, charged out too. Fists started to fly, which was no good to me because I was right in the firing line.

I needn't have worried though as Jock nearly knocked me out when getting past me to throw haymakers and with Cramby's flying karate kicks we more than held our own. The two new boys had certainly come in handy that night.

It was a crazy end to the night, and it was a feud that would rumble on when we played each other again at Gigg Lane in April.

After the Carlisle defeat we went on a poor run where we only won twice in eight games, taking just nine points out of a possible 24. This run would be the difference between us finishing in the automatic promotion places and the play-offs.

It was the first time in my Bury career where I feel I struggled for form. Like the previous season I had started every game, and since joining the club had played over 100 consecutive matches. I was feeling tired and probably did need a rest, but I was headstrong and kept telling the manager I was fine – but deep down I knew my form wasn't great.

The first match in this run was away at Torquay and it was a game that didn't help my heavy legs as we had to play 40 minutes with nine men.

Terry Dunfield was the first player to see red when he handballed on the line and Torquay took the lead from the resulting penalty. We equalised soon after when I teed up Chris

Billy to drill one home from 25 yards, but early in the second half Danny Swailes, who had already been booked, pulled one of the Torquay players back and it was obvious he was in trouble.

The game carried on for ten seconds or so before the ref pulled play back and Swaz was now no longer near where the original incident happened. I quickly ran over to Michael Nelson, who was partnering Swaz at centre-half. Nelse and Danny looked similar – well, they were both tall and had no hair at the time – so I hatched my masterplan as the referee went to consult with his linesman as to who committed the foul.

'Nelse, tell him it was you or we're down to nine here,' I said.

'Fuckin' hell yeah,' Nelse replied with his eyes widening. 'Ref, it was me, it was me,' he carried on almost begging to be booked as the ref walked back towards us.

We thought we had him as the ref started spinning Swaz and Nelse round to check their numbers, but it was big Danny who got his second booking and a red card, and the plan almost backfired more as the ref threatened to book Nelse for trying to con him.

Somehow, we held on for the whole second half and a 1-1 draw was a good point in the circumstances.

After the Torquay game I hadn't scored in nine so the manager called me into his office and said he thought being captain wasn't helping me. He felt that without the responsibility I could concentrate on my game more, so he was taking the captaincy off me.

I didn't agree with what he said. I was not playing particularly well, but I didn't think that was due to being captain.

Nelse took over the armband and as a vocal centre-half he was a more natural choice. He was an organiser, a brave defender, already had the respect of the lads and would go on to lead the team well.

Although I no longer had the 'burden' of being captain I still wasn't scoring goals even though my form was beginning to return. We beat Bournemouth at home but then lost to Rushden

& Diamonds and Bristol Rovers before returning to winning ways with a 2-0 home victory over Lincoln City, thanks to a double from George Clegg.

We then played Oxford United at home and drew 1-1. I had an outstanding game, and it takes a lot for me to say that. Outstanding in every aspect expect one – putting the ball in the back of the net.

I made a goal for Cramby with a great run and cross and ran Oxford's back line ragged but I missed two great chances, one of them an absolute sitter, and I was getting a bit of stick from the crowd who were getting frustrated with my lack of goals.

The local press got it spot on in their report when they gave me man of the match and wrote, 'It would be churlish to just focus on Newby's failings in front of goal as he was the best player on the pitch by a mile.'

It was no consolation, though. I hadn't scored in 14 games despite still making a lot of goals. At the time I would have taken two goals and being the worst player on the pitch by a mile.

We then lost 3-1 away at Darlington at their old Feethams ground. What a leveller that place was – I wouldn't have ever fancied going there in the FA Cup with a Premier League team.

After that came the long trip to Exeter in early April and despite my lack of goals, I was playing with confidence after the recent performance against Oxford.

The first half was eventful to say the least. Within 30 seconds I found myself clean through only to smash my shot against the keeper's legs. Ten minutes later I was in again and bent the ball round the keeper to score and end the drought – and I was away celebrating, sprinting the length of the pitch to the away end where my brother was.

I was already over the halfway line with half the team chasing me when I heard the repeated whistle of the referee and turned to see the linesman waving his flag for offside. I'd intercepted a back-pass. How could I be offside? But it wasn't me who the linesman had raised his flag against. As I shot, Lee Connell had been standing in an offside position. He hadn't even tried to touch the ball and just watched it fly a couple of yards to the side of him on its way into the goal.

It was a ridiculous decision, but I was brought back down to earth with a bump and I thought I'd never score again.

My eventful half continued as I whipped in a left-footed cross for Chris Billy to give us the lead. Ceebs returned the compliment five minutes later when he hooked the ball over Exeter's back four and my pace got me there before the keeper. I hit it low and hard into the far corner.

Not even a dodgy linesman's decision could deny me this goal. Both relief and joy swept over me. The drought was over.

As I wheeled away to celebrate, I saw Preecey charging down the touchline Mourinho-style towards the corner flag to jump on me with the lads. I don't think it was just the fact I'd scored, but more that he wouldn't have to listen to me moaning any longer. We went on to win 2-1 and for me it was the perfect day.

The following week our feud with Carlisle reopened. The game itself was poor with our friend Foran scoring a superb late equaliser, volleying into the top corner in a 1-1 draw.

Carlisle had played in our dark blue third kit from the previous season as they had only brought their white away kit, despite the fact Bury had played in white shirts for the last century.

They reluctantly agreed to wear our kit after moaning for an hour that we should be the ones to change so that they could have their own badge on their shirts. It was obvious they had planned it in an attempt to unsettle us.

There were very few handshakes between the players at the final whistle as there was real bad blood between the two teams. What happened shortly after the game left a really bad taste and was not something I'd seen in football before.

They showered and changed quickly and were away from Gigg Lane in record time. Next minute there was a knock on our dressing room door from one of the Bury YTS lads whose job it was to sweep out the away dressing room after a game. He had with him the pile of Bury shirts that Carlisle had just worn for the game. They would never be worn again, though, as they had all been cut in half with a pair of scissors.

Preecey was fuming and if they had still been at the ground there would likely have been another rumble like there was in the tunnel up at Brunton Park.

We then had two games over the Easter weekend, first travelling to local rivals Rochdale for the derby on Good Friday. I used to love playing at Rochdale as Bury always took a massive following there and outnumbered the home fans. It made for a great atmosphere.

As someone who's followed my team all over the country before I played, I know how special those away days are to the supporters. Those trips are the ones you remember when you're looking back on the good times. As a fan, even if you lost the day was still special, as you felt you were there representing your club.

It takes nothing for us as players to go and clap those supporters in the away end after the game to thank them for travelling hundreds of miles to watch us and it used to make my day as a Liverpool fan when the players used to come over and celebrate a win with us – so I always made sure I applauded those who travelled to support us.

It was a massive day out for our supporters on their derby day, and many used to actually walk the six miles from Bury to Rochdale, stopping at every pub en route. No wonder our fans were so vocal on those trips to Spotland.

We put in a good performance and won 2-1 with Nelse scoring a great header and Cramby calmly slotting home a penalty.

We then hosted Scunthorpe United in a dour 0-0 draw, although it's one I really remember with the last couple of seasons catching up with me physically.

It was my 108th consecutive start and I remember Billy Ayre saying to me just before the start of the previous season that if I made as many channels runs and closed down defenders as much as I did then I would be burnt out by Christmas. He had been right, I was burnt out, but I'd at least made it to Easter the following season – so about 16 months longer than he originally thought.

I can even remember the exact time that I hit the brick wall in the Scunthorpe game. Midway through the second half Nelse carried the ball out of the back line and went on a great run, beating four or five, and then played it wide to me. I tried to go past the full-back and I felt like I was running in treacle.

I had no change of pace, no next gear to go in to and for the first time in my career I felt physically exhausted.

We had two league games left and then were probably going to end up in the play-offs, as we needed a lot of unlikely results to go our way to finish in the top three. I would just have to fight through the tiredness and hope I would be rewarded by us getting promotion.

We travelled to Southend and were excellent in a game which secured our place in the play-offs. Nelse scored yet another header and even though Southend equalised I delivered a cross from the left early in the second half that Lee Connell met and scored with a great header to give us the win.

The very least we deserved that season was a place in the play-offs and it looked like we would play Bournemouth or Lincoln City. Our final-day defeat at home to Wrexham meant that we would be playing Bournemouth over two legs and they were the toughest opponent we could have.

The first leg of the semi-final was at home and was to be refereed by Premier League official Jeff Winter.

I had never been massively impressed when I'd seen him on televised games and seeing him live didn't change my opinion of him as I thought he'd got a major decision wrong.

Bournemouth's right-winger Wade Elliot elbowed Jamie Stuart on the stroke of half-time as they both jumped for a header, breaking Jamie's nose in the process. Instead of Elliott being punished, Jamie was shown a straight red card for pushing Elliott to the floor in anger at having his nose rearranged.

If the ref was sending Jamie off then Elliott surely had to go with him, but it was only a yellow for the Bournemouth man and we had to play the whole of the second half a man down.

We held on to draw 0-0, but the momentum was all with Bournemouth going into the second leg three days later when we would have our left-back missing through suspension while Elliott, who was Bournemouth's best forward player, was free to play. Still, Winter seemed happy with himself, even signing autographs for fans after the game.

I was interviewed after the match and said it was a massive blow for us to be without Jamie for the second leg and should we make the final he would miss out. As he had been one of our most consistent players all season he wouldn't deserve that.

The next day at training he thanked me for supporting him and for what I'd said, but in my opinion, I thought he'd been hard done by and the video of the incident backed that up.

The away leg was always going to be tough, and I was annoyed on the morning of the game by an article in the local press claiming I wanted to leave. I had done an interview with the paper at least ten days before saying as I hadn't yet been offered a contract it could be my last few weeks as a Bury player, but it was the same for a lot of players.

I'd had a decent season, scored 12 goals and assisted a similar number, and although my overall form hadn't been as good as the previous season, I had scored more goals and had again started every game, 54 in total. There aren't too many players who will start every single game in two consecutive seasons and it's something of which I'm very proud. I thought that the timing of the article, on the morning of our biggest game of the season, was disgraceful, with fans questioning my commitment.

That was the one thing that annoyed me more than anything – the fact that people were questioning my commitment. It still hurts to this day.

I had started every game since I had joined Bury except two, in April 2001, when I was recovering from an ankle injury. I'd started 122 games in just over two seasons – 110 consecutive starts since damaging my ankle at Oldham. I had played with injuries, I had turned down a move to Oldham when their chief executive bad-mouthed the club, I knew of bids from Blackpool and Wigan and never kicked up a fuss or asked to leave and still people wanted to question my commitment.

I couldn't understand that and never will. I wanted to stay at the club no matter what league we were in, but I was hoping for it to be League 1.

The game itself was a disaster as we lost 3-1 and looked tired after playing half a game days earlier with ten men. Preecey came on to grab a late consolation, but it was a difficult night, and the dressing room was deathly quiet. I felt numb, mainly because, with the club staying in League 2, it was already known that they would look to release the top earners, of which I was one.

I didn't want to leave and had already spoken to the manager, telling him I was willing to take a pay cut to stay. Deep down I think Preecey wanted to freshen things up and thought me leaving might be the best thing all round. He never said that to me, but it was the feeling I got.

I spoke to the regular press guys, Gordon Sorfleet, Phil Thorp and Keith Maddocks, after the game and they too had been disappointed that the local paper had printed the article. Print it afterwards by all means as the fall-out of the season begins but not as we are preparing for the second leg of a play-off semi-final.

It was the worst I had felt in my career. Being a footballer is the same as any job, it was just how we earned a living, but that first spell at Bury never felt like a job to me. I was desperate to succeed, for myself yes, but also for the club and the supporters. I had one supporter say to me not long ago that he felt I 'got Bury'. I think he was right. The place just felt like the perfect fit at that time in my career.

Bournemouth eventually went on to beat Lincoln City 5-2 in a one-sided final and although it means nothing, had we got to the final I honestly think we would have beat Lincoln as, although they were a big and physical team, their lack of mobility at the back would have been perfect for our pace on the big pitch at the Millennium Stadium.

The season, however, was over, and after 122 games and 24 goals for Bury I looked all set to leave the club.

7

I don't have many regrets from my career but ...

I DON'T have many regrets from my career. I would have liked to have played at a higher level for longer, but as for decisions I had to make there weren't many I wish I hadn't taken.

The one regret I did have was signing for Huddersfield Town, and I don't mean that in a detrimental way. They were and are a big club, but I had a nightmare season for them where simply nothing went right, and I honestly don't think there were any positives to take from my year at the McAlpine Stadium.

The start of the 2003/04 season was the beginning of a three-year period that was by far the toughest of my career.

I had no choice but to leave Bury, the reason being that I simply wasn't offered a contract to stay. Once it was determined that Bury were staying in League 2 a few of us were told that our contracts were too expensive and if we wanted to stay then we would have to take significant pay cuts.

I had no problem with that as every business, football club or otherwise, has to cut their cloth accordingly. Nobody really wants to take a pay cut in any walk of life, but I loved Bury and didn't want to leave so I wanted to speak to them about what the lower offer was going to be. No offer ever came, so I found myself on the PFA list of released players.

I was more than hopeful of having a fair amount of interest after the way I had played over the last couple of seasons.

Rotherham United's assistant manager John Breckin rang, wanting to know what my wages were, but football wasn't even mentioned, and I never heard from them again. Oxford United manager Ian Atkins called and offered me an almost identical deal to what I was already on. However, he wanted an answer there and then and I didn't want to rush into anything.

QPR's Ian Holloway rang to see if I would be happy to move down south. 'Where do you live now?' he asked. 'Not far from Southport,' I answered

'Long way from the seaside is Loftus Road,' was all he said in reply. We agreed to keep in touch over the close season but there was no concrete offer of a deal.

The other two clubs to make firm offers were Colchester United and Huddersfield.

Huddersfield were looking to totally rebuild in League 2 after being relegated and coming out of administration. I went to speak to them and was impressed at what manager Peter Jackson and Terry 'Taff' Yorath had to say. Jacko was a larger-than-life character who had been a hero at the club as a player, and Taff was a very experienced man in football having played for and managed big clubs.

I knew the money wouldn't be what I had been getting at Bury as the club were just recovering from a financial crisis which had nearly seen them go bust. The move appealed to me, though.

Huddersfield were a big attraction with a great stadium and averaged over 10,000 supporters at home games. Although I wasn't delighted with the money, I agreed a two-year deal and felt that the Terriers could be where I kicked on.

At the time I was staying with my girlfriend Wendy in Bury. I would bump into fans and they would tell me I was greedy for not staying at Gigg Lane. I never said anything to them at the time, but it infuriated me. I couldn't stay at a club that didn't want me to stay, could I? I never refused to sign a new contract. I simply wasn't offered one.

I was taking a wage cut of over £500 a week to sign for Huddersfield yet I was being called greedy.

Although no contracts could be signed due to Huddersfield's precarious financial situation, a lawyer's letter was drawn up with the agreed terms and I shook hands on the deal with Peter Jackson, so as far as I was concerned it was done, as that was how I worked.

The following day, however, I got a phone call from my old Sheffield United team-mate David 'Ned' Kelly, who was now assistant manager at Tranmere Rovers, a division higher than Huddersfield; he said that they would have taken me straight away.

I had shaken hands, though, so as far as I was concerned, I was a Huddersfield Town player. Looking at the situation now, I should have gone back on my word and gone to Tranmere. That was the biggest regret that I had from my career. If Jacko had realised how my season at Huddersfield was going to go and known of Tranmere's late interest, he would probably have driven me to Merseyside himself.

Pre-season at Huddersfield was by far the hardest of my career. It was horrendous. Our training ground backed on to the woods and we were constantly running up the hills there and didn't see a ball for weeks. It was an absolute slog, but Jacko wanted the fittest team in the league, and he got it.

When the friendlies started, I couldn't stop scoring. A goal in my first game at non-league Wakefield. A goal and an assist for Lee Fowler in a really entertaining 3-2 win at near neighbours Halifax Town at The Shay, and I then put one in the top corner against Championship side Sunderland in a 2-0 win at the McAlpine – but that was as good as it got.

It was always going to be a tough start as we had a totally new squad. A lot of the players from the previous season had moved on and at least 12 new players had joined, so it would take the new team time to gel.

The strikers were Jon Stead, of whom big things were expected, and experienced fan favourite Andy Booth. The manager also brought in experience in Efe Sodje, Ian Hughes, Steve Yates and Tony Carss, while there were some good young players who were ready to play first-team football, so there was a good mix.

The season's opening league game was at home to Cambridge United on an unbelievably hot day. At pitch level the heat was almost unbearable. The game finished 2-2 with Stead scoring both of our goals and Dave Kitson netting Cambridge's pair. Both men would go on to play many games in the Premier League for various clubs.

I was satisfied with my league debut, setting Steady up for his first goal, but I knew it was vital to get off the mark early at a new club just as I had at Bury. It took so much pressure off you as a striker.

We then beat Championship side Derby County 2-1 in the League Cup, when I did well, and travelled to Boston United for another 2-2 league draw.

With half an hour left we were trailing, and I was moved out to the left wing as Boothy was brought on to partner Steady and provide more of an aerial threat. It was probably the best half an hour I had for Huddersfield as I beat my full-back and got crosses into the box at will and Boothy won nearly every ball.

In the end we just couldn't find a winner, but before I'd even got off the pitch at the end of the game Taff came running over saying he'd counted nine crosses I'd put into the box in 20 minutes, and that I could be a real threat out wide; he gave me a pat on the back.

It was his way of saying that Steady and Boothy would play up front while I'd be playing wide in the next game at Doncaster Rovers. And I was.

The only problem was that I had a nightmare at Doncaster. It took me 59 minutes to beat my full-back and even then, I pulled the cross five yards behind everyone. My number went up a minute later and I had no arguments.

It had been a difficult start to my Huddersfield career but at least manager Peter Jackson had backed me in the local press, saying, 'In pre-season and the first couple of games, Jon looked really sharp alongside Steady, and I know they like playing together, but Jon also did really well when he first went out on to the wing, allowing Boothy to play up front, and it's a shame it hasn't worked out for him in the last couple of matches.

'He works his socks off. He will chase lost causes all day and the only thing he needs now is a goal. Once he gets one, he will go on and get plenty because he's got pace and a great ability to finish. I'd be delighted for Jon if he could do that because he works extremely hard, and he has shown a great deal of loyalty to me and to this club.

'He could have signed for seven other clubs in the summer, but he chose Huddersfield Town on a letter of intent and he could have walked away at any time as the offers came in. That says a lot about the lad.'

After the draw at Doncaster, we beat Bristol Rovers 2-1 at home in a game I was surprised to start, and next up was my first return to Gigg Lane to play Bury.

It wasn't a trip I was looking forward to, especially after the rubbish that fans had been fed in the local press for the entire week building up to it, and I knew the reception I was going to get off fans who once loved me wasn't going to be good.

I was right. It didn't affect me during the game, but it did afterwards. I was hurt by my every touch being booed by the majority of the Bury crowd. Getting stick didn't bother me, and I actually used to enjoy it when playing for Bury against the likes of Wrexham as it made me more determined to score so I could give them a bit back, but I thought that the reception the fans gave me that day was wrong considering the effort and work rate I'd put in for their club over the previous 122 games.

Even Andy Preece said that he thought it was the wrong reaction from the supporters. It hurt more because deep down I still wanted to be there playing for them.

We lost 2-1 and the Huddersfield fans weren't happy. They were a passionate and vocal crowd and followed the club in big numbers. They were expecting promotion back to League 1 and we had only won one of the first six games.

I hadn't really performed yet and that day I was the scapegoat. I was the first to admit I wasn't playing well, but neither were a lot of other players. It's not often that someone gets booed by both sets of supporters, but I did that day. And it hurt.

Peter Jackson spoke to me at training on the Monday and said he had already decided to leave me out for the Northampton game at the weekend as he felt the fans getting on my back wasn't helping me or the team.

I had no problem with him leaving me out as that's probably what my performances deserved, but I didn't agree with him bringing the fans in to it. That was just an excuse. I wasn't going to hide from a few idiots in the crowd.

I started a few weeks later in a 1-1 away at Rochdale where I made our goal, crossing for Jon Worthington to head home, but I was playing with little confidence. I was also starting to struggle with a knee injury which felt a bit more than the usual aches and pains. I had been doing a lot of driving as at the time I was splitting my time between my house near Formby and my girlfriend's in Bury, and when I got out of the car in the morning after driving my knee would be unbelievably stiff and sore.

Once I had warmed up, I could just about get by, but sprinting was agony. During a training session before we travelled to Southend I turned and my knee nearly gave way. It was becoming a major worry for me.

When we arrived in Southend we had a bit of a loosener in a local park after the long journey and Jacko, who never wanted to be seen as boring, decided that whoever gave the ball away most in the circle had to do a forfeit and do a lap of the park in just their boots and socks.

There was a bit of cheating going on but Nathan Clarke ended up the unlucky loser. Clarkey, however, was not the shy or retiring type and seemed to enjoy it. His finest moment came when he stopped to go through his groin stretch repertoire against a park bench that an old couple had just sat down on, and when he returned to the rest of us his kit had disappeared courtesy of one of the lads.

I was on the bench at Southend as expected and it was a good job as the long journey had made my knee worse. The manager told me to warm up with about 20 minutes left and as I was attempting to jog up and down the touchline all I could think was, 'Please don't put me on, I can't run!' I was hardly going to get back in the fans' good books in this condition.

We won 2-1, but the result was the last thing on my mind and after speaking to the physio it was agreed I would travel to Sheffield to see the club surgeon the following week. After the consultation the surgeon was confident it was a routine cartilage tear and the operation would be done the following week and keep me on the sidelines for about a month, so it wasn't too bad at all.

However, when the surgeon opened my knee up he found it was much worse and once he had trimmed my cartilage he found I also had a partial tear of my anterior cruciate ligament. I was looking at three or four months out and some major rehabilitation work before I could play again.

He said I had been very lucky not to have suffered a complete rupture as I'd been playing with it for the last couple of weeks. It was a massive blow; the best-case scenario was that I wouldn't be fit until mid-January.

It was a long 14 weeks but my rehab went well, and our physio Lee Martin worked me hard and kept me going.

My day would normally consist of cardio work in the morning on the bike and rowing machine and then some really hard work on the electronic thigh and hamstring strengthening machines we had at the gym next to the stadium. After dinner it would be straight into the swimming pool for an hour. There were four of us with long-term injuries and with a couple of the lads having the ability of Eric the Eel you had to choose your partner carefully for the relays – especially when you had lads jumping out of the pool to be physically sick. Those pool days were killers.

I felt really fit when I resumed full training and played in a reserve game away at Bradford City, a little bit ahead of schedule, in mid-January. I was just enjoying being able to play again and played really well over 80 minutes, scoring both goals as we won 2-0.

Peter Jackson was there and was pleased with my performance so wanted me to travel with the first-team to York City for their Sunday fixture.

After only one reserve match in nearly four months, I wasn't expecting to even be on the bench and thought Jacko was only taking me as a reward for working so hard over the last few months and for my performance in midweek. However Steady went down ill overnight and Boothy was complaining of a sore groin on the morning of the game so all of a sudden, I went from sitting in the stand to starting.

I played for 80 minutes and did well despite running on empty for the last quarter of an hour I was on the pitch and contributed as we won 2-0.

The following week we lost 2-0 at home to Darlington in what would be my last start for the club. With the regular strikers both still injured I was partnered up front by Nat Brown and made two great chances for him in the first half, but he didn't take either of them and when we went two goals behind on the hour, I was the one dragged off. I felt I was the easy option to take off.

The following week we had two away games, Torquay United on the Saturday and Bristol Rovers on the Tuesday, so rather than be up and down the motorway we stayed in that part of the country for a few days.

I was an unused sub as we won 1-0 at Plainmoor and on the Monday the club brought in one of my old strike partners, Pawel Abbot, on loan, which effectively brought my time to an end.

It was obvious that Pav was being brought in to play ahead of me, but I helped him settle in and I set up a debut goal for him the following night when we were both thrown on as subs to salvage a late equaliser at Bristol Rovers.

March of that year brought about my first deadline-day move as York manager Chris Brass took me on loan. I had done well against his side a few weeks earlier and Brassy, as player-manager, had been marking me that day.

Unfortunately York were in absolute freefall and having started well, still being in the top three in November, were on a horrendous run having taken just six points out of a possible 51, dropping into the bottom three.

When Brass came in for me I had decided that I had nothing to lose. I'd had a stop-start season due to form and injuries and at least I would get a run of six or seven appearances in the month I was at York. So, I made the dash back to the McAlpine to get all the paperwork signed and I was a York player by 5pm.

When I arrived at my new training ground the next day it was obvious all wasn't well at the club.

I liked the manager and his assistant, Lee Nogan, but there was a lot of moaning in the dressing room about training methods and team selection which is normal when things aren't going well. The players, though, didn't seem to want to take any responsibility for the situation at all and it was an 'us against them' situation between players and staff.

It was going to be a tall order to reverse the club's situation on the pitch with all of that going on. I think the manager knew all wasn't right in the dressing room and, in my opinion, he deserved better than what he got from the players in the month I was there.

Our first game was the next day and, having only just joined, I was named on the bench and came on at half-time when we were already 3-0 down and well beaten.

There was no fight and no belief in the team. I remember my brother waiting by the team coach after the game for a chat and just before we left Brassy came over and told me I would be starting against Macclesfield Town the following week.

As we spoke, I introduced Brassy to my brother. The manager said to him, 'You haven't got any boots, have you? Bring them next week; you can play instead of some of them.' He was fuming and from what I'd seen so far, I could understand why.

Macclesfield were also in and around the relegation zone, so the next game was a big one. I started on the right of midfield.

I was desperate to play up front but it was just nice to get a game. I played well, picking up the man of the match award afterwards – but we lost 2-0 and once the first goal went in some of the lads were too quick to give up.

There were some decent players too. Darren Dunning was an excellent technical midfielder and Darren Edmondson was an experienced right-back. Brassy himself was at centre-half and Liam George, a former Luton Town favourite, was up front. But confidence was low all over the pitch.

The next game brought a further defeat away at Cambridge, after which the manager told a few home truths in the dressing room and said there would be changes for the next home match – which saw my former club Bury come to Bootham Crescent.

Graham Barrow was now manager at Bury after Preecey had left in December of that season. Graham pulled me aside in the corridor before the game asking me what the situation was at Huddersfield and if I thought they would let me go for free in the summer. Free? Jesus. I think they would have paid Graham to take me off their hands!

He told me he wanted me back at Gigg Lane and it was a boost to hear he rated me as a player. A move back to Bury certainly appealed to me.

As the opposition manager he probably shouldn't have told me before the game as it gave me a massive boost. I played well against my former club and made the equaliser in a 1-1 draw, setting up Liam George – another former Bury player – to score at the end where the visiting fans were stood. The pair of us couldn't resist celebrating right in front of them.

We were better than Bury on the night and deserved to find a winner. It had been my first start up front and my best performance for York, which was no coincidence, but we were running out of time to stay in the division. Draws were simply no good.

We had to beat Yeovil in the next home game to give ourselves hope and, despite taking an early lead through Darren Dunning, the familiar frailties resurfaced and we lost 2-1 condemning ourselves to relegation barring a miracle. I got another man of the match award, but I was too disappointed to bother going to any sponsors' lounge after the result to pick it up.

Relegation was confirmed with another defeat at high-flying Doncaster Rovers. I had experienced the sinking feeling of the drop and failure again. It was horrible.

I returned to Huddersfield with the season slightly extended as the club had missed out on automatic promotion by conceding with just six minutes left on the final day at Cheltenham Town. A tricky play-off semi-final against Lincoln City was just about safely negotiated, which set up a final against Mansfield Town at the Millennium Stadium.

I had spoken to Jacko and Taff about the possibility of leaving in the summer, despite having a year left on my contract, and if the club and my agent could agree on a settlement then I would be free to go. We all agreed it would be the right decision for both parties.

Sometimes it just doesn't work out at some clubs and Huddersfield Town was one for me. I didn't look to blame anyone else. It was down to me to succeed and I hadn't done that.

Despite doing well in the opening league games I hadn't managed to do what every striker going to a new club needs to do and that was get on the scoresheet, and my form and confidence suffered as a result.

I still maintain that had I scored early in the season my time at Huddersfield would have been very different, so that outcome was even more frustrating after such a free-scoring pre-season.

I had no problem with Peter Jackson or Terry Yorath, apart from the murderous pre-season hills. They had both done a great job that season and we parted on good terms while Huddersfield went on to win promotion by beating Mansfield Town on penalties to head back to League 1.

I went to Malta the following day for my brother's wedding and left my agent to deal with the settlement.

After Huddersfield had gained promotion, my contract was worth just over £60,000 for the next season and their first offer for me to leave was £5,000, so my agent's attitude was, 'Well, if you're going to be silly then so are we,' and asked for £55,000.

The cat-and-mouse game of offers went on for a week or two and in the meantime I had more or less agreed a deal to return to Bury.

My Huddersfield contract was eventually terminated for somewhere in the middle of those two figures and I was heading back to somewhere I hadn't wanted to leave – but the emergence of a future England international and another serious injury left me thinking the saying 'never go back' was true.

8

What's the old saying? Never go back

THE MOVE back to Bury seemed the right one at the time and I was excited to be returning to Gigg Lane.

Due to the tax-free settlement from Huddersfield, negotiations were fairly swift and I signed a two-year contract on just over £40,000 a year.

Graham Barrow was someone I liked; he was tough but fair. I'd worked with him before and I thought he could get the best out of me, but his assistant Kelham O'Hanlon made it clear he didn't rate me from the moment I met him.

Basically, he told me in the first conversation we had that he didn't think I would get in the team. It was my job to prove him wrong and he was entitled to his opinion, but we got off on the wrong foot from the very start and the two of us never really saw eye to eye.

The manager, however, seemed happy to have me back at the club and made his point in the local press, 'I'm delighted to get Jon Newby back. I've always got on with Jon and when I took my first training session when I started here, it was Jon who stood out above the others. The quality stood out a mile. After that he probably played every game for the club while he was here.

'He's a manager's dream, really. He is always fit, always available and long may that continue. He is a quality player and knows there are more goals in himself. He had other offers from clubs, better offers, but he wanted to come back to this club and I think that is a massive plus for everybody.

'I hope to use Jon in a way that makes the other players use him better. We will never stop him breaking from centre to wide areas, that is his game, but the number of times he got behind defenders to find there was nobody there was ridiculous. He got behind defenders more times than I have ever seen any player do and we need basically somebody who can keep up with him.'

Graham wanted experience for this league and brought in Dave Challinor, David Flitcroft and Graham Jones along with skilful midfielder Brian Barry-Murphy and young centre-half John Fitzgerald.

Jones was a striker and along with me, there were four other players vying for those forward positions – David Nugent, Chris Porter, Simon Whaley and Colin Kazim-Richards, all of whom would go and play at a much higher level.

The squad reminded me a bit of what had happened at Huddersfield the summer before. A lot of players came in, with three more towards the end of pre-season in Lee Duxbury, Dwayne Mattis and Paul Scott, and it was going to take time for the team to gel.

The opening game of the season was at home to Yeovil. Every player is desperate to start on the first day and I was no different.

The day before, I went over on my ankle. I got through training as we weren't doing much other than walking through a bit of team shape and I thought I would be fine the following day when I'd be lining up on the right of the front three.

When I woke up in the morning I was still struggling, but after the nightmare season just gone I didn't want to miss out on any more football. I should have been more patient as I knew my ankle wasn't right to play. I got a strapping on it and played, and it was the wrong decision. I struggled, not just because of my ankle, but it played a big part.

We were 1-0 down after an hour when Dave Flitcroft and I were replaced. Five minutes later we were 2-1 up thanks to two David Nugent headers and Flickers turned to me on the bench and said, 'Fuckin' hell, Newbs, we'll never play again after this!'

He was joking, of course, but it would be two months before I started another league game. We went on to win 3-1, which was a great result for the team, but for me it was a miserable start to the season.

Nuge started the season with two goals and his performances that season were outstanding. He had been a youngster getting the odd game when I had originally been at the club and although very quick, he was still finding his way. The change in him when I returned was massive.

He had gone from a boy to a man in that year and he looked a real player. He went on to have a great career at the top level, even playing and scoring for England.

I liked the way he played even as a youngster, always busy and looking to make things happen. He didn't give defenders a minute's rest and had so much energy; we could see that he would be a big player for us that season.

In the matches that followed I would normally get on for 20 minutes or so on the right or left of a front three with the instruction, 'Don't let the full-back run past you.'

It was difficult playing in that position in a struggling team. If you are Mo Salah or Sadio Mané playing for Liverpool then a lot of your defensive work is in the opposition's half, high up the pitch, but in a struggling team without the lion's share of the possession you end up playing as a wing-back or, if the full-back is someone who goes forward a lot, you end up as almost a second full-back.

I did so much defensive work in my own half, which as a centre-forward is difficult when I wanted to be at the other end of the pitch, running channels, receiving the ball with my back to goal in the penalty area and getting behind defenders. They were my strengths.

I couldn't do that from such a position, especially when my role was as rigid as stopping the full-back.

There was no rotation – it was almost straight lines up and down. I was always criticised for not scoring enough goals, which would be fair, but I saw myself as almost a 'second' striker who would get ten a season playing up front and if I played with an out-and-out goalscorer I would create another ten for them.

In my first spell at Bury I scored 24 goals but I also made 26, which is a lot of assists, and I just felt I would always be far more effective playing in a two as a centre-forward.

My frustrations continued, as did my 20-minute spells on the pitch. We drew 2-2 at Bristol Rovers and then lost 5-1 at Grimsby in a game where they were awarded two penalties in less than a minute. Glyn Garner saved the first but from the resulting corner a second was awarded for handball, which they scored.

We were unbelievably inconsistent, and our first ten games resulted in three wins, three draws and four defeats, leaving us with just 12 points out of a possible 30. Improvement was very much needed.

I finally got my second start of the season at home to Macclesfield and played up front with Nuge in a two.

We fell behind early to a goal from future team-mate Matthew Tipton, who had a great goalscoring record in the lower leagues, but it wasn't long before we got back on level terms, thanks to my first goal back at the club and my first for 12 months.

A long clearance by our goalkeeper was misjudged by the Macclesfield centre-backs and left me in a 50-50 challenge with the keeper. Having not scored in so long I would have knocked my own granny over, never mind the opposing stopper, and I took the ball almost out of his hands to side-foot home.

When the ball hit the net I'd almost forgotten how to celebrate, but there is a great picture of me just screaming with relief. It was a massive weight lifted from my shoulders and I played as though as I was free. I went on to have a really good game and made a late winner for Nuge – and to me it was no coincidence that when I played up front in a pair, I had much more of an impact.

I started the next match at Leyton Orient, which we drew 1-1 in what was a decent away point. After that it was back to the boredom of the bench and I just couldn't get a long enough run of games to secure my place in the team.

Results were still very inconsistent, and we were in the bottom half of the table despite having the form player in the league that season in David Nugent.

My next start was away at Northampton, again up front with Nuge, in the last game of 2004. We were under pressure for long periods but looked dangerous on the break and twice I got away in the left channel to make two great chances for my strike partner, but unfortunately his normal deadly radar was out by inches as he hit the post and the bar.

We went on to lose 2-0 and I was taken off after 70 minutes, but I was more than happy with my performance and thought I was unlucky to be subbed.

Had the two efforts that saw Nuge hit the woodwork been an inch the other way I would have been given praise for making two goals.

As it was, in training as we prepared for the New Year's Day game at Lincoln, I found myself not involved in the team shape, meaning I wasn't in the starting line-up – and I was pissed off. A few of us were sent over to the physio Joe Hinnigan to do some ball work and I didn't bother giving it my best.

I had never kicked up a fuss when I was left out at Huddersfield or earlier in that 2004/05 season for Bury, as my performances meant I hadn't deserved to start. I was always very honest, probably too honest in my own assessment of how I played. This time I didn't agree with Graham's decision and it was probably the first time in my career when my attitude had been wrong. I went through the motions in the training session with the physio.

I regretted it afterwards as that wasn't my style, and I apologised to Joe the next day on the team coach on the way to Lincoln, where we lost 1-0 – and I didn't play a minute.

The defeat was a bad start to the year and we also lost David Nugent, who was sold to Preston North End that month. His goals and his energy would be a big miss.

We signed Andy Keogh on loan from Leeds United as his replacement and I partnered him in attack as we lost 3-2 at Scunthorpe United.

Andy and I linked up well and looked like we had the makings of a good partnership as we played together again at home to Northampton Town, when we both scored. My goal came as I robbed a defender in his own half and slotted the ball into the corner to give us a first-half lead.

I then started the next six matches and just as myself and Andy were looking a genuine threat together, he was recalled by Leeds and sold to Scunthorpe on a permanent deal.

Graham then loaned in forward Bas Savage and, although players at that level are often inconsistent from game to game, this fella was inconsistent from minute to minute.

One minute he could bring the ball out of the sky on the end of his toe like Ronaldinho but the next he would trip over the ball. Playing up front with him, I had no idea what he was going to do next – and I'm not sure he did either! He made a big difference, though, with a lively second-half showing as we came from 2-0 down at Boston United to draw 2-2, and I grabbed the equaliser after racing on to a through ball from David Flitcroft before sliding it under the keeper for a valuable point.

We were then shocking, losing 3-0 at Rushden & Diamonds, and Graham was coming under pressure from the fans as we slipped towards the bottom six. We were prepared right by him, but we just weren't performing and that was down to us not him.

We travelled to Southend on the Friday and that night Chall and Flickers called a players' meeting where we agreed that

Graham was under pressure and we desperately needed a result for him. He was a manager both liked and respected by the majority of the players and I had a good relationship with him. I liked him as a person, and we had an honesty between us.

I was never the type to go knocking on a manager's door when I wasn't in the team. I knew if my performances were good enough to warrant a starting place, and I would rather question myself than the manager if I wasn't playing. When I was left out, I always felt that working hard in training and scoring goals in the reserves would get me back in the team, not knocking on the manager's door.

Graham had always been fair with me and apart from the Lincoln game I don't think he really got my place in the team wrong.

A few home truths were said at the meeting, when players got things off their chest, and we were determined to get points on the board at Roots Hall.

Graham changed things around a bit with me on the left, Bas Savage down the middle and Colin Kazim-Richards on the right. Col was a good player. He was only young, but he had everything that was needed to play at the very top.

The one thing that was questionable back then was his attitude. He was marmite in the dressing room, you either loved him or hated him and a lot of his team-mates probably fell into the latter of those categories. I enjoyed having him there because there was always something going on with him and we got on well.

I liked his confidence and loved the fact that for someone so young he wasn't afraid to challenge the senior players in terms of having an opinion and, because he could play, he backed it up.

He had a swagger about him and an ego which was often taken for arrogance, and in some ways back then it was. Yet some of the things he did and the goals he scored in training were outrageous.

He would go on to play in countries all over the world and play for some top clubs. He always had that natural ability.

I remember him trying to nutmeg Dave Challinor in training once in a two-v-two exercise and for the next few minutes Chall forgot about the ball and whacked Col up in the air countless times.

The young lad didn't go missing, however, and kept asking for the ball and trying to take Chall on. Every time he got kicked, and Chall didn't half get into him, he just got up. No fuss, no moaning. He just demanded the ball again, and I remember thinking, 'Fair enough, kid, you'll do for me.'

He was never going to win any popularity stakes in the Gigg Lane dressing room, but the young lad could play, and he knew it.

The meeting didn't change our fortunes as we lost 1-0 at Southend and I felt I was wasted out wide after my recent good performances through the middle. It looked like we were heading for a relegation battle.

Our next home game was a massive one as it was against Cambridge United, who were in the relegation zone, so it was almost a 'must-win' fixture.

Graham decided to go with three up front again and I wasn't one of them. I was bitterly disappointed, but it actually worked in my favour. We went 1-0 down midway through the half and for the first half an hour we were absolutely awful. Bas Savage was playing wide right and was really struggling with the position. The supporters were starting to get on his back and 35 minutes in Graham had seen enough so made the brave decision to make a change that early in the game, even telling me he had made a mistake as I stood on the touchline waiting to go on.

I was sent on and made an impact straight away, giving the team more pace and getting a couple of dangerous crosses into the box, and the fans got a bit of a lift as we looked much more of a threat going forward.

We were the team looking most likely to score in the second half and ten minutes after the break an intelligent Chris Porter header set me up to put a half-volley into the top corner past Cambridge keeper John Ruddy and bring us level.

The goal gave not just us, but the fans, energy. They really got behind us, and we got a priceless injury-time winner when Flickers smashed one in from 25 yards.

That gave us some breathing space from the relegation zone and showed both the fans and the directors that we were fighting for Graham, as we celebrated the winner by the whole team jumping on him on the touchline.

We then went to Yeovil in the next game and won 1-0 in a brilliant team performance where I kept my place after my goal against Cambridge.

However, despite going into the home match with Grimsby feeling good after recent performances, it was the start of the most frustrating and painful 12 months of my career.

The game started really well. I made an early goal for Chris Porter, Brian Barry-Murphy added a second and we were well on top.

Grimsby had Justin Whittle at centre-half, a real competitor, and I enjoyed playing against him. I had some good battles with him over the years at Stoke, Hull City and Grimsby and there was a real mutual respect between us.

I had just chased a ball into the channel and tried to sprint away from him when I began to feel a dull ache on my heel, which was getting worse every time that I put my foot down. I couldn't get anywhere near full pace and was in a lot of pain even at half-pace.

I was gutted and had to come off.

We went on to win 3-1 but I was really down as there was no obvious swelling and I hadn't been kicked, so it was a bit of a mystery injury.

The injury hadn't settled down after a week, so I was sent for a scan which showed some wear and tear in my ankle joint. One of the doctors thought there was the possibility of having a bone spur, which is when an extra piece of bone starts growing on the outside of a joint.

It was decided I would have an injection in my heel and then rest for a week to try and solve the problem, but seven days later there was no improvement at all – if anything it was worse. I had a further scan and this time the club surgeon looked at the results and said there was a large bone spur on my Achilles, so I would need an operation to remove it.

By now we were in April and the season was drawing to a close. I ended up missing the last nine matches, of which we won three to finish 17th. The final game was a 1-0 home defeat to Swansea City, who needed a win to gain promotion. Their fans took up three sides of the ground and then half of the pitch as they scored in the first 30 seconds in what was a fantastic atmosphere.

The operation on my heel was just before that game, in the first week of May, and all being well I should have been fit to start pre-season training in the first week of July 2005.

I was also getting married in the first week of June and I was under strict instructions from the Mrs that she didn't want me hobbling down the aisle on my crutches!

The operation was a success according to the surgeon and I was in at Gigg Lane three days a week throughout the summer to help with my rehabilitation.

Our physio, who had some of the best stories I've ever heard from football over the years, was a great fella to work with, but we just couldn't get my recovery right. It wasn't a simple injury. It had been major surgery and not a typical aftermath that Joe had dealt with before.

Even after my wedding a month after the surgery I was still in a lot of pain and my Achilles tendon at the bottom of my heel was twice as big as it should have been. We were on our honeymoon in America, and I took to filling a bucket from the ice machine at the end of our hotel corridor three or four times a day to try and ease the pain and swelling.

Pre-season was fast approaching for the 2005/06 campaign and I was heading into the last year of my contract, looking like I wasn't going to be fit enough to start the new season, which was a major worry.

9

I don't think I'll ever get fit

OVER THE summer, Graham Barrow had brought in some experienced players in the shape of goalkeeper Neil 'Taff' Edwards from Rochdale, and former Premier League strikers Stuart Barlow, once of Everton, and ex-Watford man Allan Smart.

Chris Porter had departed for Oldham Athletic after an impressive season and Colin Kazim-Richards, the 'Coca-Cola Kid', had left for Brighton after the drinks company ran a competition allowing a fan to win £250,000 for their club to buy a player.

Another departure was assistant manager Kelham O'Hanlon. He wasn't someone I was particularly sad to see go.

Staff aren't always there to be liked, they are there to get the best out of the players, and there was no doubt that Kelham was a good coach and very knowledgeable about the game.

He didn't rate me and made that clear, but by the end of the season there were too many players who didn't get on with him and I'm not sure the manager had a great relationship with him either. Ray Mathias, a very experienced coach and former manager, was brought in to replace Kelham.

I was still miles off playing or even training due to the ongoing problems with my heel, and there were even discussions with the surgeon about me going under the knife again and having another operation.

He was adamant, though, that the operation had been a complete success and even showed me the large piece of bone he had shaved off my ankle to try and reassure me. It was hoped that the issue was simply that the scar tissue following the surgery hadn't been broken down enough, so for a week I had Joe the physio digging his fingers and thumbs into my ankle three times a day for 20 minutes. I wouldn't wish it on my worst enemy!

It was a good job his stories were so funny, because the treatment was agony and I used to leave the physio room with a sweat on and sore fingers where I'd been gripping the bed so hard.

It was worth it, though, as the swelling began to go down and I was able to start some light jogging, which was a major boost, even though it was exactly three months since the operation, so I was well behind schedule.

The first game of the season was away at Cheltenham, and despite taking the lead through new signing Dwayne Mattis, we lost 2-1. Three days later, in our first home match, Leyton Orient beat us by the same score.

The Gigg Lane crowd weren't happy after just two games of the season. They hadn't been overjoyed with the appointment of Graham as they had wanted a clean slate from the Andy Preece regime, and at times if felt that no matter what team Graham picked, he could do no right by sections of the support.

I had started training with the team the day before the Orient game and after that defeat, the manager asked me if I felt fit enough to be involved at home to Shrewsbury Town the following weekend. I was full of energy and sharpness in training, as players so often are after a long-term injury. When we come back we are just happy to be back playing football and the adrenalin is flowing again.

I told Graham if he needed me to play I would. I felt good despite the fact I would only have been back in team training for just four days after being out for more than four months. It was unheard of, but it shows what lower-league football can be like.

There were no sports scientists or injury performance analysts like there are now monitoring the returning players in training. Squads were small and sometimes you had to be thrown in before you were ready.

The team was struggling, and Graham felt it might even give the crowd a bit of a boost if I was back. I wasn't as popular with the Bury fans as I had been in my first spell at the club, but some still held me in high regard and the manager thought me coming on late in the game might help the supporters get behind the team.

It was 0-0 when Graham gave me the nod to go on just after the hour and it proved to be a great decision as it took me just nine minutes to open the scoring.

It was a collector's item, too, as it was a header. Allan Smart swung in a deep cross from the left, Dwayne Mattis nodded it back across goal and I threw myself forward to score with a diving header from six yards out. A few months of frustration came out in the celebration that followed.

I didn't score many headers and a young Joe Hart in the Shrewsbury goal can always tell his grandchildren that Jon Newby put one past him. Little did I know then that it would be the last goal I ever scored for Bury.

As the game entered the final minute I had a sore groin and hamstring after being thrown back into a league game with such little training, but Brian Barry-Murphy scored a superb goal to secure a 2-0 win and the risk to play had been worth it. I had more than played my part in helping the team to our first three points of the season.

We definitely needed more goals in the team, though, as Graham so far had mainly left Stuart Barlow on the bench and had already nearly come to blows with Allan Smart after a dressing-room argument.

The manager moved to sign Matthew Tipton, which I thought was a great signing. Tippy had scored goals for Oldham and

Macclesfield at that level and would be a popular signing with the fans.

I never had a problem with managers signing players in my position. It was up to me to prove I was better than them or deserved to play alongside them. Tippy came in and was just what the dressing room needed. He was bubbly, confident and an opinionated character. He was experienced and knew the game and the two of us got on straight away.

He came to Bury as he had fallen out with Mansfield Town manager Carlton Palmer, but Palmer didn't want him to leave and apparently told Tippy, 'You can go to Bury if we can have Newby in return.' It was at least nice to know that other managers still rated me.

Tippy went straight into the team the following day for our home game and made an immediate impact by scoring our second equaliser in a 2-2 draw at home to Wrexham.

I had rounded the keeper in the first half to give Brian Barry-Murphy a tap-in for our first goal of the day, but I was disappointed to miss a chance when through on goal in the second half as I put it too close to the keeper.

A few days later we lost 1-0 at Macclesfield, despite absolutely battering them. Their goal lived a charmed life, and the result was made worse by us having a last-minute equaliser wrongly ruled out from a corner for a supposed foul by me on the keeper when the referee told our captain Dave Challinor, 'Newby was moving about too much in front of the goalkeeper.' That was a new one on me!

After a slow start to the season, Graham was under pressure again. We then lost 1-0 at home to Carlisle – which was a game too far for me. After five starts in a very short space of time following my long lay-off, and not much training, I pulled my hamstring quite badly late on and I was frustrated to be back on the side lines again for a month.

The next two results didn't go our way and after training one Monday in September, Graham was unfortunately relieved of his duties. We were gutted for him. He was always very fair with us while at the same time demanding, and throughout his period in charge at Bury, he always had the respect of his players.

He asked to see five or six of us in his office individually before he left. The two of us spoke for five minutes and wished each other all the best. It was a sad day for us as players; Graham was a good manager and a good man and there were a few tears from some of the lads he had worked with for a long time over the years.

Youth team coach Chris Casper took over on a caretaker basis. He had been at Manchester United and Reading before a terrible injury had sadly ended his playing career.

He started his time in charge with a narrow 2-1 defeat at Oxford United. I was still injured at the time but travelled with the squad and did the radio commentary with long-serving club press officer Gordon Sorfleet, which was a side of things that I enjoyed while I was out injured.

We then beat Bristol Rovers 1-0 and a week later drew 1-1 at home to Lincoln City, where I returned from injury for the last half an hour and did well enough to start at Rushden & Diamonds the following Friday night.

We put in a really good performance at Nene Park and scored two second-half goals to win. It was my first start under the new manager and after a decent opening to his caretaker role he was given the job on a permanent basis.

I had felt really good in the game and there was no hint after the game of what was to come the following day when we were due in at the club for a warm-down.

As soon as we started, I knew I was in trouble. I was having the same pain in my right heel as I had in my left heel against Grimsby, which led to my operation for a bone spur. Everything was the same. The more I ran the worse the pain felt, until I couldn't even put my foot down.

I could feel myself sweating out of sheer panic and my heart was pounding. I didn't need a physio or a scan. I just knew. It was as low as I'd ever felt in football.

I'd worked so hard to get fit after a few difficult seasons. I could hardly bring myself to tell the physio. I was sent to the same surgeon and a quickly organised scan proved what I had feared. The diagnosis was another bone spur, this time on my right heel.

I was operated on the next day and that Rushden & Diamonds match proved to be my final start for Bury.

The aftermath of the operation was slightly different than previously in that I had a blood drain attached for a few days. I didn't think anything of it at the time, but when I came to have my stitches taken out, the wound half-reopened and looked a mess.

I could deal with it looking so bad as I didn't have the most attractive feet anyway. But it didn't just look a mess, it felt a mess.

After a month of the wound being open, as apparently re-stitching it would have run the risk of an infection, I was again in as much pain as before the operation. Both rehabilitations had been average to say the very least.

The club would moan at me that I wasn't getting back to fitness quick enough, yet I didn't have the treatment I needed, and I told the club exactly that.

I would be sent up to a local gym every day to work on my own, or with another injured player. I could motivate myself to work hard, that wasn't a problem, but when you are coming back from another long-term injury and you're still in pain you need people pushing you on and getting you through it. I didn't get that.

Joe had left his role as physio a few weeks after Graham Barrow's departure and for a short period, we had different part-time physios coming in to treat us. They had never worked in a busy professional football club before, which was fine for normal everyday knocks, but for players coming back from difficult surgery and whose rehabilitation was complicated it was a big disadvantage in terms of trying to get fit.

Things came to a head in the December when the club were now simply guessing as to why my foot was still so swollen and sore. At one stage they even thought I had gout.

I still had a hole in my foot and there was no light at the end of the tunnel. Chris Casper came to the physio room to ask me to go to a carol service at a local church to represent the club that morning as opposed to getting treatment off the physio, and I lost my head and had a go at him, shouting down the corridor at Gigg Lane. I didn't want to go to a bloody carol service, I wanted to get fit after – apart from that brief month of games – being out for the best part of ten months with two identical injuries that hadn't been managed properly.

At one stage I went to a faith healer. That's how much it got to me. Nothing had worked and we were researching anything that could help, and alternative medicine was mentioned. I lay there chuckling to myself and rolling my eyes as the woman claimed she could cure me by placing her hands an inch above my ankle for half an hour. That's how desperate I had become.

Things only started to improve when the club appointed physio Nicky Reid. He was brilliant and like any good physio saw it as his mission to get me back playing.

He worked me unbelievably hard, both in the gym and in the physio room, but I had complete confidence in what we were doing. There were setbacks along the way, as every time I tried to join in training I would have to drop out after half an hour as my heel became too sore; the manager was getting fed up with me breaking down every time I returned to the pitch. I couldn't blame him. The team were struggling and in danger of becoming involved in another relegation battle so he wanted all his players fit.

Finally, the doctors found an infection in my foot – it had only taken them two months – and at last I could work towards training again.

The mood and morale in the squad wasn't what it could have been. The manager had his own way of doing things, which was only right as it was now his team. On a Thursday we would have a vote among the players for who had been the worst player at training that week and on a Friday, if it was you, you'd have to bring in a few packets of biscuits, then we'd have a couple with a cup of tea before training.

A lot of clubs did something similar. It wasn't like you were eating a whole pack of chocolate digestives, just a couple while you had a few laughs as a team. Chris, as was his right as manager, didn't like this and told Flickers he would prefer us to change the biscuits to fruit. I can still see the look of disgust on Flickers's face as he came bursting through the dressing room door after being called into the manager's office. 'It's fuckin' fruit Friday from now on, boys,' he wailed, with a shake of his head.

The change didn't go down too well. A couple of the senior players weren't having it and decided we would train and then have the little get-together after training instead. Stuart Barlow used to hide the biscuits in the unused sauna at the back of the home dressing room at Gigg Lane.

I had been at the club for over two years in my first spell and had been back at Bury for about 18 months but I had never seen that sauna switched on. Not once. Yet the first time Stuey hid the biscuits there we came back to three packets of melted chocolate digestives and a roasting-hot sauna. There was a spy in the camp somewhere over 'Biscuitgate!'

I finally returned to training and, although I was happy to be back, I felt off the pace. I was lucky that I was never a player who put weight on, but I was miles away in terms of fitness and match sharpness through no real fault of my own. I made three very brief substitute appearances in March of that season, my last coming in a 1-1 draw with Oxford United. I was nowhere near fit. I touched the ball three times and gave it away three times. It was the last time I put on a first-team shirt for Bury.

As deadline day approached the manager told me that Kidderminster in the Conference wanted to take me on loan. At first I said no as, although they had very recently been a league club, it would have been my first drop into non-league football.

I had no future at Bury, that had been made clear, and I wouldn't be offered a new contract. After nearly three injury-hit seasons I had to put myself in the shop window for the following campaign, so I changed my mind and agreed to make the move for a month.

It was the wrong decision. I should have seen the season out at Bury as I wasn't fit enough to all of a sudden be playing a lot of games over the Easter period. Added to that, my wife Wendy was pregnant with our first child and with her in and out of hospital with issues linked to her pregnancy, it wasn't the time for me to be living away from home a few days a week.

My debut for Kidderminster was a local derby away at the old-fashioned Edgar Street ground of Hereford United. We won 1-0 and, although I hadn't started a game for seven months, I lasted for 70 minutes and did well, feeling surprisingly sharp. It went downhill from there.

We were beaten, sorry thrashed, 5-0 at home to Grays Athletic and then drew 0-0 at home to Stevenage in an uneventful game. A trip to another of my former clubs, York City, finished in a 2-2 draw in what was by far my best appearance for Kidderminster.

The only other thing I did of note during my month at Aggborough was miss a penalty away at Dagenham. I was a sub and went on at half-time with us 3-0 down. We got a penalty during the second half and I thought that as I had been out that long with my injuries, I needed to remind other managers that I actually still played. What better way of doing that than by getting my name on the scoresheet.

The problem was that I missed as Dagenham's keeper, the ex-QPR man Tony Roberts, pushed my shot on to the post.

It summed up the season, if not the last three seasons, and I'd had enough of football. I had got to a stage where I'd started to hate the game. The move to Kidderminster had been the wrong decision and I had fallen out of love with football.

I was officially released by Bury the week after and for the first time in my career I wasn't expecting the phone to ring in the summer.

10

Where do I go from here?

THE PHONE simply had to ring, though, as I became a father for the first time in May that close season.

On 22 May my wife Wendy gave birth to our son Josh. I wanted my boy to watch his daddy play football at some stage.

Josh was in hospital for a while after he was born and even while he was recovering from an early illness, I drove up to York to speak to their manager Billy McEwan after impressing him while playing for Kidderminster in that 2-2 draw. I spoke to him at length but there was no way I could travel to York five times a week and be a full-time player on part-time money, so I had to forget about that one.

The only other call I had was from Darren Ferguson, who was still a player at Wrexham and had been for the last six or seven years.

I had done well against Wrexham over the years and Darren had told his manager Denis Smith to have a look at me, so on that advice I was invited in for a trial.

I had only been there for two days when Graham Barrow, who was now assistant manager to Mark Wright at Chester City (who like Wrexham were in League 2), called me to ask me to go and play for Chester in a game against Stoke City the following night. Wrexham advised me to go as they had only just come out of administration and there was no guarantee I could be offered a deal even if I impressed them.

It was a difficult time as I went from new dressing room to new dressing room trying to fit in and make an impression. At the top level, football is very glamorous but as a player in League 2 who is out of contract it is anything but, scratching about trying to find a new club in order to make a living.

I was at Chester for about two weeks, and it was a bizarre time. The match against Stoke went well for me but in the dressing room before the game there were 26 outfield players so I thought it would be a result just making it on to the pitch.

I started up front with Jonathan Walters and had a very good 45 minutes, so I felt really positive.

Graham rang me the next day to tell me the chairman Stephen Vaughan had been impressed and they wanted me in to train and play more games.

I trained and worked hard and played in the next match at Conference side Droylsden, where I scored the only goal and was a threat all night. The only problem was that Mark Wright wasn't even there.

Graham said to me after the match that I looked 'back to my old self' and I knew if it had been his decision then he would have signed me. He relayed back to the manager how well I had done, but his words seemed to fall on deaf ears. I had been in on trial on Graham's say-so, not the manager's, and despite me doing so well in the two games there was no offer of a contract.

So it was back to the drawing board, but fortunately there was a practice match organised at Wrexham's Racecourse Ground as an open day for their supporters during the final week of pre-season. I was invited to play in that.

My performance was average to be honest and I wasn't expecting to be offered anything by Wrexham, but I was. Denis Smith offered me a month-to-month contract on £500 a week and before he even got the words out of his mouth I said yes!

It was typical that I had gone on trial to Chester City and done really well yet wasn't offered a deal, only to be offered a contract by Wrexham having been average during my period there.

Interestingly, my Wrexham debut came in the derby at Chester. If I was in any doubt about the passion of this fixture, then the police escort all the way from Wrexham to Chester made me realise how much it meant to the supporters. They hated each other and the atmosphere in the ground was poisonous.

I was named a sub and got a bit of stick off the Chester fans as I warmed up during the first half, as did every Wrexham player, but one supporter started giving me abuse for choosing the Welsh side over his and I had to smile at that one as I carried on stretching.

It was ironic that for the last few years most fans had given me stick for signing for their club, but this fella was having a go at me for not signing for his!

We won 2-1 with local lad Mark Jones and captain Neil Roberts, a fans' favourite and great pro, scoring our goals, and it was a great game to be a part of – even when Chester's Roberto Martinez nearly broke my leg late on with a terrible tackle.

No wonder I enjoyed those two 4-0 Liverpool victories against his Everton side so much from the Kop!

My first game at home was against league leaders Swindon Town, and I was reminded by a few of our supporters about the incident in which I was accused of making a gesture at Wrexham fans while playing for Bury, which led to me being booed by them ever since. I have to say that the Wrexham supporters were brilliant with me in my time at the club and although the team was struggling, I never felt they were on either my or the team's back.

I played for 85 minutes against Swindon due to an early injury to Robbo and I had my best game for Wrexham as we won 2-1. I had a hand in the moves that led to both our goals.

Dennis Smith seemed pleased in the press with his comments, 'Jon did well when he came on. I have known him since he was at Liverpool and thought he would be a very good player, though he has had spells with injuries that curtailed that. But at this level he is a threat. If he performs like he did on Saturday I will be happy.'

I had to play well, though, to make sure I got another month's contract. I kept my place in the starting line-up away at Accrington Stanley and, despite having played so well when beating Swindon, we were dreadful in losing 5-0. The next match wasn't much better as we lost 5-2 at Stockport County, where I made a goal for one of my former Liverpool team-mates, Danny Williams.

We then played Bury at Gigg Lane in November and, although I was only on the bench, I was desperate to get on and prove a few people wrong.

We were 1-0 down at half-time when the manager told me I was going on, and I felt that 45 minutes would be long enough to make an impression. Within 45 seconds being introduced I knocked the ball past my old team-mate John Fitzgerald in the channel and knowing Fitzy wasn't the quickest, I did him for pace. As I got to the byline and put my cross in, I felt my hamstring go pop and almost burst out of the back of my leg.

It wasn't just a little tweak or overstretch, it had gone in a big way. I felt sick. I'd had an injury-hit season to end my time at Bury and I'd been back on the pitch less than a minute and I was injured again.

I dragged myself off the floor slowly and walked back to my position. There was no way I was going off the pitch to get the 'I told you he's always injured' shouts. Not a chance!

For the next 45 minutes I somehow got myself through the game. Nobody could tell I was injured despite the fact I was almost dragging my leg with me in absolute agony.

We lost 1-0 and when we got back in the dressing room the bruising was already starting to come out in the muscle. I made up some story about it happening in the last five minutes, but I think Denis Smith knew. I couldn't even get out of the car when I got home. The physio Mel Pejic said we were looking at a six-to-eight-week lay-off, but my contract ran out in ten days.

The club secretary Geraint Parry was brilliant and, despite the fact that Wrexham were struggling financially, he said that as I had got injured playing for the club my contract would be extended by another month on the same money, so they could help me get back to full fitness. I was very appreciative of that as the club could have released me when my initial contract finished.

That further month ended in early December and I had only just started some light jogging by then, but the club had signed another striker on loan and there was no money left to give me another deal, so in order to just get fit and injury-free I stayed on after signing a month's contract for the minimum amount of money that a club is allowed to offer a professional, £90 a week.

I had no choice. I needed to get fit so that I could find a new club, but I wouldn't be fit until into the New Year. I worked so hard with the physio in the three weeks leading up to Christmas and then the club and I parted ways and I had no idea where to turn next.

11

Going through the motions

I TURNED to the place where it all began, the park. I ran to the park every morning. I did shuttle runs using the pitches there. I took a ball with me and did football movements to try and keep sharp. It was soul-destroying. Dogs would run over and try and nick the ball. A few of them reminded me of defenders I had played against over the years!

I got a call off my former Bury team-mate Dave Flitcroft, who was assistant manager at Rochdale and knew I was training on my own. He told me that he and Keith Hill, the manager, were more than happy for me to go and train at Rochdale. It was perfect for me as I was only living 15 minutes away from their training ground.

I was only there for two weeks, but the training was brilliant. It was sharp, physical and very intense. The work ethic was as good as anywhere I'd been, and the staff were really positive about everything they did. Possession, finishing; all the players loved it and I was no different. I got to play in a reserve game at Wrexham of all places and scored one and made one in a 3-1 win.

Peter Davenport, the manager at Conference side Southport, was watching and got in touch a day later to offer me a deal so I signed for his club until the end of the season, hoping it would be a stepping stone to getting back in the Football League. Although at 28, once you had fallen into non-league, it was extremely hard to move back up again unless you were promoted – and that wasn't going to happen with Southport.

I was straight into the team after one training session and we were beaten 2-1 at home to Forest Green Rovers. I made a goal for Sean Patterson and hit the bar late on.

Southport had some decent players, but two stood out – Carl Baker and Mark Duffy, both of whom had signed from Liverpool club Prescot Cables, and both would go on to have long, successful careers in the Football League. Bakes was mesmerising at times when he had the ball and was far too good for the level he was playing at.

My only goal for Southport came the following week, a header as we beat Altrincham 2-1 at home. I found Southport a strange club at times. We trained at the park behind the Haig Avenue ground, yet the council kept kicking us off the football pitches. Which town's council kicks its own football team off a football pitch in a public park? The pitch at the ground wasn't in great condition so on some days we would run through the streets of the town, on the beach or around the lake at the marina.

When we did train, it felt like the senior players took the sessions rather than the manager. Peter Davenport was fairly quiet and a decent man but there just didn't seem to be much authority – as though he didn't want to upset the players.

I had played non-league football at Kidderminster but it had been run like a professional club, whereas Southport just wasn't like that. I had no problems with training at the park, I didn't have any airs and graces about me like that, but even if you were playing for the Dog and Duck there has to be some authority coming from the top.

The manager, however, did show his authority away at St Albans City, who were at the foot of the table. Southport were trying to beat the drop and we were 2-1 up going into the final minute away at a relegation rival when our keeper Paul Harrison, a great lad and former Liverpool player, came and took a great catch from a free kick to take the pressure off us.

As he got up, he thought he heard the ref's whistle for a foul and put the ball down to take a free kick. Except it wasn't the ref's whistle he had heard, and the opposition striker simply tapped the ball into an empty net. We dropped two points.

If the manager had been quiet up to that point, he wasn't two minutes later when we got back to the dressing when he nearly woke the dead with his five-minute rant at Paul. I think after four months of him biting his lip at some of our performances, it all came out in those five minutes and even now the incident makes me laugh.

By the time the season finished I was only a sub and not enjoying football at all. I didn't see the point in playing if I was going through the motions and I wasn't enjoying it, but since leaving school football was all I had known.

It was a tough summer as Southport were a part-time club. Most part-time clubs only pay footballers for 40 weeks, and Southport were no different.

It had been the most difficult four years of my career and things could only get better.

12

I was back in the Football League

I WROTE letters to a lot of clubs and managers that summer, but I was the forgotten man.

I had a call off Jim Vince, who was manager of Northern Premier League side Witton Albion, in the seventh tier of English football. I've never had the attitude of being too good for anyone so I thought I would go and train with Witton. At least I would be keeping myself football fit if any trials did come along later in pre-season. The training was great, a breath of fresh air from what I'd known at Southport, and Jim and his assistant Nigel Deeley were professional in every way.

A couple of weeks into July I had an offer from Morecambe to go and train with them and I really fancied it. They had just been promoted from the Conference for their first season in the Football League.

Sammy McIlroy was the manager with Mark Lillis as his assistant. They had both been heroes on either side of Manchester in their playing days and had a lot of experience, and there was a good feel about the club as soon as I got there.

There was no long-distance running during pre-season; everything was short and sharp and then it was straight into ball work. It worked for the players as pre-season was injury-free and performances were good.

My first appearance came against Barnsley. I played for 45 minutes as we won 2-1 and I scored soon after going on at half-time. We then played Scottish First Division side Morton, winning 3-0, and again I scored and made a goal.

I was enjoying my football again, while there was a real buzz about the club after the success of the previous season. I enjoyed the training and the lads had made me feel welcome and, after my initial performances, I had gained their respect early which was so important.

The club had signed my former Southport team-mate Carl Baker in the summer for what was a lot of money for Morecambe, and he would be a big player that season. He was another striker but I was confident McIlroy would offer me something with the way things were going.

He called me in to his office about ten days before the season kicked off to say the club wanted to offer me a year's contract, but the money would be low as there was nothing left in the budget.

The money wasn't massively important at that stage and I was almost skipping out of his office. I got into my car and just let out a roar. Not only was I signing for a club moving forward but I was back in the Football League.

I felt I deserved to get this contract. I had worked hard over the last few years and after some terrible luck with injuries I deserved a little bit of good fortune for a change.

Morecambe were not big payers but during the conversation it was made abundantly clear that if I took my chance and had a good season there would be a better deal the following year – and I couldn't argue with that. It suited me and was an incentive to be successful.

Our last pre-season game was away at the club I'd just left, Southport, who were still managed by Peter Davenport. I came on at half-time to make the only goal with a strong run and cross and even Davenport praised me after the game. Well sort of.

'I knew it was in there somewhere, Jon,' he said while shaking my hand after the game, referring to the fact that I hadn't really done it for him. I had just showed him, though, that I was actually a decent player.

The terms of my contract were actually sorted out on the Southport pitch after the game with the Morecambe chief executive, although I was about to ring Jim Vince and sign for Witton Albion after his first offer.

We eventually agreed a deal very similar to what I was on at Wrexham. I was one of the lowest-paid players at the club with the established players on double my wages, but I backed myself to do well and earn the better deal both the manager and chief executive had told me would be there the following season.

It was a lively dressing room at Morecambe with a real mix of characters. 'Mr Morecambe', Jim Bentley, was in charge and was a real leader. He was always eventually going to manage the club one day.

Long-serving striker Wayne Curtis was a big personality, along with fans' favourite Michael Twiss, and box-to-box midfielder Craig Stanley.

There were also some quality younger players. Simon Grand, who signed at the same time as me, was an excellent centre-half, and despite still being relatively young had plenty of professional experience at Carlisle and Rochdale. Then there was Scott Davies, an upcoming young goalkeeper, and Paul Lloyd, a lively winger who kept the lads on their toes with some of the stuff that used to go on in the dressing room.

Lloydy was hilarious. He was one of those players who everybody liked. The stories of his antics at the weekend made sure I got in early on a Monday just to listen to him! He had you in the palm of his hand. I just wish he would write his own book so I could relive a few more of his tales. Players like that are priceless in dressing rooms.

A few years later I was playing for Andy Preece again at Northwich Victoria and Preecey, who knew I had played with Lloydy at Morecambe, asked my opinion on him as he had the opportunity to sign him. I recommended that we signed him as he was a very good player – but deep down, I just wanted to hear his stories again!

Our first game of the season, and Morecambe's first game in the Football League, was a disappointing goalless draw at home to Barnet with me coming on for the last ten minutes. It was uneventful but at least we had a point on the board in a season where we were favourites to go straight back down.

I was then on the bench for our next league match away at Wrexham, but we found ourselves 2-0 down at half-time. It wasn't good for the team but it was good for me as the manager threw me on at the break.

It took me just 11 minutes to get on the scoresheet, side-footing home after good work by Carl Baker. It was the first league goal in Morecambe's history.

The Racecourse had always been a lucky ground for me as an away player. I had scored there for Bury, Bury's reserves, Sheffield United's reserves and now Morecambe, making it seven goals in seven appearances. If only I had scored that many for Wrexham, then I needn't have had to bother to go to places like St Albans City and Gravesend & Northfleet with Southport!

After the Wrexham game we drew 1-1 at Notts County, conceding a very late equaliser, and we then travelled to Championship side Wolves in the League Cup after disposing of Preston North End in the previous round.

Molineux was as impressive as ever and this time there was no Kevin Muscat to kick me all over it, so that was a plus point.

Sammy McIlroy liked to play with just one up front, normally Matty Blinkhorn, with Carl Baker and Twissy either side of him. As well as those three there was Garry Thompson, Wayne Curtis and myself, so there was plenty of competition for places and the manager had assembled a good squad. Wolves away was always going to be one up front so, as expected, I started on the bench.

We went 1-0 up through a Carl Baker penalty and passed the ball about so well, as so often happens when a lower-league club go and enjoy playing at a big stadium with a pitch like a bowling green. We were pegged back with just 15 minutes to go when Wolves scored a penalty of their own and I got the nod to go on just after the equaliser, but the game finished 1-1 and we headed into extra time.

In just the second minute we cleared a corner up to Blinks on the halfway line. I had been defending in our box but took off to support our lone striker who did brilliantly to get just outside Wolves' penalty area. I continued my run, and the ball was laid into my path just inside the penalty area and I passed it into the corner with the ball squeezing under goalkeeper Graham Stack.

We were 2-1 up and I had my second goal of the season. Garry Thompson added a fine third and we won 3-1 to cap a magnificent night for the club.

In the space of a few months Morecambe fans had seen their club win at Wembley to get in the Football League and beat Preston and Wolves away from home in what had been some start to the season for us.

We had another good month of results, beating Tranmere 1-0 in the Johnstone's Paint Trophy, when I made my first start for the club. We followed up that success with victories against Mansfield, Chester and Hereford and an away point at Peterborough United.

Although I had only made one start, I already had two goals to my name and had also scored in both games that I had played for the reserves.

It was enjoyable playing for the reserves as well and we worked hard. We had a core of players of myself, Grandy, Lloydy, Scott Davies, Jamie Burns and Gary Hunter who, like myself, would be in and out of the starting XI for the first-team.

The manager rarely came to the reserve games and Jeff Udall, who took the team, wasn't even a full-time member of staff, but he made it enjoyable. We would warm up for ten minutes before a game and then he'd ask if we were ready. That was it. As players we almost took the team ourselves.

We didn't lose before Christmas and, despite being under the cosh in long periods against much bigger clubs, we just couldn't stop winning and christened ourselves the 'Invincibles'.

I felt as sharp as I had done in years and there wasn't even a hint of an injury, despite the Sunday league-style ten-minute warm-ups. I was the happiest I had been in football since my first spell at Bury.

My next start in the first-team was against Port Vale, who were a league higher than us. It was another Johnstone's Paint Trophy tie and, despite playing well, we found ourselves two goals down.

We turned the game around in the second half, and I scored the equaliser as we came back to draw 2-2 and take it to penalties. With my confidence high I put my penalty in to the top-left corner and we were through to the next round to face Hartlepool away.

We were again trailing at half-time but were awarded a penalty early in the second half and with Carl Baker not starting nobody seemed to want to take it, so I put the ball on the spot.

Hartlepool had giant goalkeeper Jan Budtz between the sticks, all 6ft 7in of him, but I sent him the wrong way, putting the ball in the bottom-left corner to bring us level at 1-1.

For the second round running the tie went to penalties and we scored every kick to go through. It is always hard taking more than one penalty in a game, but if you have scored the first then confidence is always high for the second and although I went the same way, to the keeper's right, this time I went high into the roof of the net for another successful effort.

The last time I had two penalties in a game I missed them both, against Lincoln City, so it was nice to get 100 per cent in the right way!

After playing so well at Hartlepool up front in a two with Michael Twiss, the manager kept faith with the same formation for our next game away at Grimsby Town in the league.

We took the lead in the first half as I chested down an Adam Yates pass and lobbed the keeper from the edge of the box for my fifth of the season. It was one of my favourite goals of my career. Twissy added a second and we won 2-1. As a team we played with freedom and, despite being in and out of the side, which was purely down to the different tactical formations we played, I felt under no pressure to perform as I was scoring goals in whatever system I was asked to play in and I was believing in myself again after three difficult seasons.

The next game was a big one for me as we were welcoming Bury to Christie Park. They were still managed by Chris Casper and I felt I had things to prove to people at that club.

The local press asked me to do a preview and I said how much I was looking forward to the game, but I also reiterated that I had felt let down by how the club had dealt with my heel injuries and that for the last few months of the season the manager hadn't really spoken to me.

We played really well and deservedly won 2-1, which took us in to the top ten of the league table. My only disappointment had been hitting the crossbar with a left-footed volley after Jim Bentley had headed a corner back across goal.

As I walked off the pitch, I saw Casper waiting by the tunnel and put my hand out to offer a handshake. He refused and followed me up the tunnel ranting about me lying in the press the previous day.

In the end, after a few verbals, big Jim got in between us and we probably both breathed a sigh of relief, as I don't think a fight between Chris and me would have registered much in the heavyweight division!

I started at Brentford in a good 1-0 win, but after a 2-0 defeat at Wycombe Wanderers where I hardly got a kick I was back on the bench for the games early in the new year. One of those was again at home to Bury in the Johnstone's Paint Trophy and I wasn't the only player happy to be on the bench that night. Morecambe is cold enough in the summer, but in January when the rain and golf ball-sized hailstones were coming down sideways in a force nine gale, the bench was definitely the safest place to be.

We led 1-0 at half-time due to a Matty Blinkhorn header and the score was still the same when I went on with ten minutes left. Bury were chasing an equaliser and pushing men forward, leaving plenty of space at the back, and in the last minute a long ball over the top gave me a chance. I skipped past my old mate Colin Woodthorpe's sliding challenge and rounded the keeper to score and to secure our place in the next round.

All this rubbish about not celebrating against your former club, I've never really understood. Bury was the club I wanted to score against more than anyone, apart from Everton! They had released me twice in my career and I wanted to remind them I was a good player.

As much as I had loved the club, that goal against Bury was one of the most satisfying of my career for obvious reasons. I and Chris Casper also grew up a bit that night and shook hands before we went down the tunnel.

From a Morecambe perspective, we were in to a two-legged area final against Grimsby with the winner destined for Wembley.

The next few games were in a strange period for me. It was the first time the manager had all six strikers available at the same time, so it was obvious that some of us had to miss out. After the Bury match we lost our next two without scoring and I sat on the bench for the full 90 minutes in both. I had scored four of my six goals coming off the bench that season, so I found that strange in itself.

The following weekend we played Notts County at home and McIlroy called me into his office before the game to tell me I wasn't even going to be a substitute.

I looked at him a bit puzzled and asked him why. His answer was that I had been doing well, there wasn't really a reason and I would be back in the squad the following week. I just looked at him with a puzzled look on my face when he said that, and he carried on by saying that he was also speaking to the club about extending my contract for another year.

It was as though, to get himself out of a situation that he wasn't particularly comfortable with, he would try and drop good news into a bad news conversation. I took it with a pinch of salt as I knew when Grandy had been left out of the squad in previous weeks he had been offered a two-year extension, never mind just the one.

Only Carl Baker, with ten goals, had scored more than me and at that stage of the season Bakes had started nearly 30 games. I had started eight and scored six. I had also scored the same amount for the reserves. It was as though there was a pecking order and no matter what I did I would be at the bottom of it.

We drew 1-1 against Notts County and although I was back as a sub the week after, just as McIlroy had said, I sat unused on the bench for three games.

There was a running joke among the lads about team selection as we rarely knew the side until around an hour before kick-off when the team sheet had to be in. There was a television in the dressing room at Christie Park, which we used to have on after a good result to see where we were in the league table, and before a home game we used to joke that it should have been broadcasting live from the manager's office, showing our squad numbers being loaded into the lottery machine, and that the first 11 numbers to come out would start. That was how it often felt the team was picked!

We were then due to play Grimsby three times in a week, twice in the Johnstone's Paint Trophy and once in the league.

We lost the first leg of the area final 1-0 at home and I came on for ten minutes. We then lost 4-0 in the league, when I started, but the manager left some regulars on in preparation for the second leg just three days later.

I found myself sat in the stand and not in the matchday squad again and to say I was disappointed would be an understatement. I was still joint second top scorer and I had only started nine games.

We were trailing 1-0 from the first leg so we surely needed goalscorers on the bench? We drew 0-0 and didn't really create anything,. I was gutted. That would be the closest I ever got to playing at Wembley.

I had scored three goals in the competition and had also scored in both penalty shootouts, and I felt let down by the manager as I missed out on trying to help the team get to the final.

It would have been very interesting had we made it to the final, as with me scoring a lot of goals to help get us there I would have been heartbroken not to be get on the pitch at Wembley.

By the time we played Darlington away in the last week of March I had still only started ten games and only had a few months left on my contract.

It hadn't entered my mind that I wouldn't be offered another one, having played well and scored goals, but I wanted to keep scoring and give the manager no choice but to offer me another deal. I was popular with the supporters as well, who had even given me my own song. The Kaiser Chiefs' number one hit 'Ruby' had never sounded so good!

I did my chances of a new contract no harm when I scored our second goal at Darlington as I met a Garry Thompson cross from eight yards to head past the keeper for my seventh goal of the season. I was taken off with 15 minutes to go but we conceded two late goals and came away with only a point.

I had done enough to start at home to Rotherham United, and we were in front early thanks to a trademark header from Matty Blinkhorn. It was 2-0 just minutes later when I beat the offside trap to fire home off the post with my right foot, and ten minutes on, we had our third and I had my second goal of the game as I ran clear to finish with my left.

Rotherham got a goal back, but it was 4-1 before half-time and a very proud moment in my career as I got my third goal and my first senior hat-trick after rising high to head a Thompson cross into the top corner.

It was the perfect treble – one goal with my right, one with my left and a header. We went on to win 5-1 and I picked up a man of the match award. The lads were delighted for me. As well as scoring the first league goal in Morecambe's history, I had also scored their first league hat-trick.

After the game, Sammy McIlroy said to the press, 'Jon has been on the fringes of the starting team all season but has always done well when called upon. He deserved a run in the team, and he is showing us all what he is capable of. He never seems to panic and in a one against one situation you would always back him. He has scored four in two games now and I am delighted for him.'

I was now into double figures for the season with ten goals in just 12 starts and I was flying, confidence-wise, yet suddenly I was really starting to worry whether I would be at the club the following season. Every time I tried to speak to the manager about my situation, he never seemed to have the time.

Our final home game of the season was a 2-1 defeat to Lincoln City, in which I played just ten minutes. The match day programme carried an interesting article which I read in the dressing room before the game. It said: 'Our ineptitude in front of goal has been well documented recently, even Sammy McIlroy has publicly acknowledged it was beginning to rile him. It was more of a shock then to watch us stick five past Rotherham recently, who in spite of their off-field problems, have still been relatively impressive this season and prior to their points deduction sat comfortably above us in the table.

'All that needed to be done was glance at the team sheet and spot "20 J. Newby" glaring back. It was his hat-trick that did the damage and the most pleasing aspect of all was that his goals were just about the only chances he had in the game.

'I mentioned earlier in the season in this column that I didn't think that Newbs had the ability to be prolific in this division. Analysing his individual stats, however, it's clear that assertion was premature.

'In all major competitions this season, Newby has started just 12 games and returned with ten goals. At any level that is a remarkable record.

'We had our best run before Christmas when Newby partnered Michael Twiss up front. Now when he is partnering Matty Blinkhorn we are seeing a return to that form.

'I think I read somewhere that he made a hand-written application for a trial with us instead of instructing an agent to issue a generic request. If true, I think it will only endear him to the Morecambe fans further. I'm convinced he has now shown enough to rival Garry Thompson in the case for contract renewal.

'I'm hoping that Thompson will be eager to continue to show just how good a player he is, setting up more goals for Newby, so we can pray that – for the love of God – they are both signed up.'

It had been a successful season for both myself and the club as we were now guaranteed a top-half finish in Morecambe's first season in the Football League.

I finally had a meeting with the manager that week and unbelievably he told me there would be no contract offer for me the following season. I was in shock. It was embarrassing as far as I was concerned.

I had finished one goal behind leading scorer Carl Baker, who had 11 goals. I had only started 14 games yet scored ten times, and I also scored the same number of goals for the reserves which said a lot about my attitude and professionalism.

I was a good trainer and hadn't been injured all season. I was on one of the lowest wages at the club, £450 a week. Not many players would have signed for that. I had kept my side of the bargain. Score goals, play well and you'll get another contract, that's what the chief executive had said to me that night stood on the pitch at Southport.

I was given the excuse that all the other forwards still had at least a year left on their deals so the only way of freeing up any money was by releasing me. I wanted another contract. I'd earned it and would even have signed for the same money just to stay at the club, which I eventually told him.

However, the manager said his hands were tied and I felt betrayed to be honest. I'd had a good season, re-establishing myself in the Football League, and I was rewarded with nothing. How could you finish as second top scorer for the first-team and top scorer in the reserves in the same season and still be released? I'd proved I could score goals. That's not a bad player to have in your squad on next to nothing.

After three nightmare seasons with a lack of form, confidence and the struggle with serious injuries I'd had a really good season yet still found myself on the scrapheap. I was devastated.

Morecambe had been good for me, but I had been just as good for Morecambe. I had enjoyed going to work every morning and I was a popular and well-respected player in the dressing room and gave my all, but through no fault of my own I had to start all over again.

13

If I scored every chance, I'd still be at Liverpool

THERE WAS some interest early in the summer from Greenock Morton in the Scottish First Division, the level below the Scottish Premier League.

It appealed to me. I had only played in England and after the way the previous season had ended, I fancied trying something new.

I spoke to the manager Davie Irons and agreed to travel to Scotland for talks. I then also had a call from Nigel Clough, who was manager of Conference side Burton Albion. Burton were still only part time despite being one of the favourites for promotion that season and I wanted to stay full time for as long as possible. I was 30 later that year but was still fit and had plenty to offer a new club.

I agreed to go and train with Burton the day before I was due to travel to Scotland, but I'd more or less decided that if my family situation could be worked out and the contract was a suitable offer then I would give the Scottish league a go.

I met the manager and the chairman Douglas Rae at the chairman's sweet factory. He was the Willy Wonka of Scottish football and rather than offer me a drink across the boardroom table he offered me a few wine gums. With my love of sweets that nearly clinched the deal there and then!

We spoke about the team and the club's plans. The manager wanted to play me up front in a two, which, incidentally, after I had signed never happened once, and the two of them both spoke well. I had a look at the ground, which was a really old-fashioned stadium, but I liked it and felt good about settling in at the club.

We then spoke about the financial side of things and there was no way I could go up to Scotland for what they were offering. I asked them what league they thought the standard was equivalent to in England and they told me the bottom of the Championship to the top of League 1 would be very similar. If that was the case, why were they offering Conference wages?

I won a bit of battle and pushed the chairman a lot closer to where I wanted to be financially and signed a one-year deal to become a Morton player, although it took me the best part of an hour to drag the last £100 a week out of the chairman.

I wanted to move up to Scotland and use a relocation fee to rent somewhere and bring my wife and son up as much as possible, but the club wanted to do something very different.

The way my week would work was that I would train with my former club Morecambe on a Monday morning, do my own gym and fitness work on a Tuesday, travel to Scotland on Wednesday and train with Morton on a Thursday and Friday, play on a Saturday and travel home on a Sunday.

It was absolute madness if any of us thought it was going to work.

There were some great lads at the club. Brian Wake, who I had played against a lot in England, helped me settle in along with Kieran McAnespie, a left-sided player who had played for Fulham and Hearts, energetic goalscorer Iain Russell, and Ryan McGuffie, a box-to-box midfielder. They were four of the biggest personalities in a dressing room in which I found the makings of a good squad.

Our first pre-season game was at non-league Threave Rovers. I was playing catch-up with just one day of training done with Burton Albion and one day at Morton, whereas the lads in

Scotland had all been back for almost three weeks with the season starting earlier than in England.

I came on at half-time to score twice as we won 9-0. We then travelled to the north-east of England and played Durham City where I was again on the scoresheet in a 3-0 win. We also played Ayr United and travelled to both of the Glasgow giants, playing Celtic and Rangers at their impressive training grounds.

We were then due to play a local team in the Renfrewshire Cup semi-final at Cappielow, our home ground. The winners would go on to play Scottish Premier League side and local rivals St Mirren in the last pre-season game. The final of the competition most years was Morton v St Mirren, due to the standard of the other teams in the competition, and in the semi-final we faced part-timers Carlton YMCA.

The manager decided that he was going to watch the first half from the stand and leave his assistant Derek Collins to take the game from the dugout. Even though we were expected to win comfortably, we played some really good stuff at a good tempo with the right attitude. I played on the left of a front three, with Wakey and Iain Russell alongside me, and we were 4-0 up going into the dressing room at half-time with everyone fairly relaxed. Davie still hadn't come down from the stand as we sat down, so Derek started to speak to the team.

It came as a bit of shock, though, when he started laying into the team about the performance being poor and 'totally unacceptable for a club like Morton'. I could see a few of the players looking round at each other a bit bemused and I was thinking, 'What's this fella on about here?' At that moment the dressing room door bursts open and in comes the manager with a big smile on his face.

'Brilliant, lads. Keep it going. We're playing some great stuff,' he said, absolutely delighted with us.

It was bizarre that the manager and his assistant could be on such different wavelengths and hadn't communicated with each other. It left Collins very red-faced and he lost a bit of credibility that day. We went on to win 9-0.

The semi-final win took us to that match against St Mirren, which was also the first time Wendy and Josh came to stay in Scotland. The game finished 1-1 and again we played well with me on the left, Wakey down the middle and Iain on the right.

Guile, strength and pace is how the manager described the front three to the press, although I'm not sure which trait, if any, he gave me!

Despite playing on the left, and I still maintained it wouldn't get the best out of me, I was pleased with my performance and I scored in the penalty shoot-out. No matter what, it's always good for a striker to hit the back of the net – although Josh didn't see his daddy take a penalty as he was fast asleep.

Our first league game of the season was away at Clyde. This was to be the first week where I would be training with Morecambe on the Monday. It was good to go back and see a few familiar faces, but also frustrating as I felt I should have still been there.

I knew my Mondays at Morecambe wouldn't last long when full-back Danny Adams decided to wind manager Sammy McIlroy up every time I scored a goal, 'Fuckin' hell, gaffer. Why did you get rid of him? He can't stop scoring!' After a couple of goals that morning I got the feeling from the manager's face every time Danny piped up that I wouldn't be asked back.

I was back up in Scotland on the Thursday to prepare for the Clyde match and as expected I was to start on the left of a three.

It was a hectic start to the game and the one noticeable thing about Scotland was that as a defender you could get away with GBH and not get penalised. It wasn't going to suit me as someone who hardly ever tackled, but there weren't many free kicks awarded despite being clattered with thigh-high challenges.

We took the lead just before half-time when a great through ball from Russell put me clean through and, despite my first shot being well saved by the keeper, I slotted the rebound in from a tight angle and I had my first goal in Scottish football.

My performance was more workmanlike rather than spectacular, but I had done a job for the team and looked like scoring the only goal of the game before a goalkeeping mistake in the 93rd minute cost us two points.

We then played Stranraer in the cup and won 6-3. I made a goal but was disappointed not to score after having a shot somehow headed off the line in the opening minutes.

Our first home game of the season again finished in a draw, this time 2-2 against St Johnstone. We were behind in the third minute but levelled almost straight away when I rounded the St Johnstone keeper and squared it for Ryan McGuffie to smash home.

Our start had been solid with two draws, but we should have won both. We won again in the cup, this time 3-0 at East Stirling, and I teed up McGuffie again for him to drive home from outside the box.

We then played Livingston and lost 2-1. I had a poor game. I felt sluggish and gave the ball away far too much in a performance that I hadn't seen coming after scoring one and making one in the first two games; I was disappointed with myself.

As I expected, I was left out for the next game away at Dundee; all five of the manager's new summer signings were substitutes that day. I don't know if that said more about his recruitment skills or the five of us as players.

It was to be a missed chance when I came off the bench that was to prove the beginning of the end for me at Morton. It was a poor game and we had created very little when I got the nod to go on with 20 minutes left.

My chance came soon after when I latched on to a weak back header. The ball bounced up nicely and I tried to lob the out-rushing Rab Douglas, but I didn't get enough lift on it and the keeper got his fingertips to it and Wakey's effort from the rebound was headed off the line. The chance was gone, and Dundee saw out the game to win 1-0.

As we got back to the dressing room, I held my hands up to the lads for not putting the chance away. The manager went mad saying it wasn't good enough. I didn't come back at him as he was right in that I should have scored.

The following day we were in for training and Davie Irons and Derek Collins asked to see me in the manager's office while captain Allan McManus took the team out to train. There was a video of the previous day's game on the television paused at the chance I missed. Irons then proceeded to play the chance over and over on the screen in front of me.

'Yeah, I should have scored, I told you that yesterday. I should have gone round him,' I said.

'Damn right you should have gone round him,' said Irons. 'It's not good enough.'

'Well, there's not much I can do about it now is there? I spoke to the lads this morning, apologised, told them I should have scored,' I replied

Again, he pressed play on the video, over and over watching the chance. The conversation continued as they said they wanted more from me. I told them they would get the best out of me if they played me up front in a two. We only had two points from the first four games, so it wasn't like the system we were playing was working.

They said I'd been signed to play in a three, despite what the manager had said to me in the chairman's sweet factory. I said although I could play better and needed to, I had still scored a goal and made a goal in the three league matches I had started and was adjusting to a more physical game in Scotland, but I was confident I could score goals given a chance.

Every time I said that the manager would press play on the video and show me the chance that I had missed the previous day. I had missed a one-on-one with the goalkeeper, not an open goal! It was a chance you see missed in the Premier League every single week by some of the best players in the world. I was merely a journeyman striker in the lower divisions, so if the best were going to miss chances like that then it stood to reason I would as well.

I had been in the office for almost an hour. I had no idea what he wanted me to do a day after the game. He pressed play on the video again and I just shook my head and said, 'If I took every chance then I'd still be playing for fuckin' Liverpool, wouldn't I?' and walked out to go and train. I even got a sarcastic round of applause off the lads, who were wondering where the hell I had been for an hour!

I was back on the bench for the cup game away at Premier League club Hibernian and, despite not winning in the league, we took a big following to Edinburgh and after being 3-2 down, I came on in the second period of extra time to play my part as we came back to win 4-3 in a brilliant team performance.

I got a phone call that week from the chief scout at Burton asking if I had any interest in a loan move to the Pirelli Stadium. I think Davie Irons had probably been on the phone asking them if they wanted to take me off his hands, but I said I'd stick it out for a few months and see what happened as I hadn't been in Scotland long.

The manager wasn't happy with the amount of travelling I was doing, and I totally agreed with him, but he and the chairman were adamant that was how they wanted my situation to be in the first place.

A few weeks later saw my final involvement at an away game at Airdrie. My wife and son were again up in Scotland and I was due to take them home afterwards.

Again, I was a sub, and after recent discussions, I wasn't expecting to get on the pitch. The first half was an absolute disaster as we went behind very early on and, when our keeper got injured, our backup Colin Stewart went on and immediately conceded a poor goal.

We went 3-0 down before half-time and the manager thought the big goalkeeper was at fault again, but I thought it was very harsh trying to blame Colin for the third goal. The manager wanted everyone in the dressing room at half-time and rightly read the riot act.

Eventually Davie turned his attention to Colin, blaming him for the goals, but Colin stood his ground about the third and eventually told the manager where to go. Now if I had a pound for every time that I'd heard a player swear at a manager or coach in the middle of a heated argument in a football dressing room, I'd have a good few quid, but Davie wasn't having it at all and began looking round for the sub keeper before realising that Colin was indeed that man!

I thought I'd seen most things in football by then, but I'd never seen a manager tell his goalkeeper he was to be sacked the next day at half-time in a game. I can still hear the manager's words now: 'That is insubordination, and you will see me tomorrow. Your contract will be terminated.'

I would have liked to have seen the keeper call his bluff and say, 'All right but I'm not playing in the second half.' Maybe I would have got a game in goal. We went on to lose 5-0 and I didn't even get off the bench.

It was a long drive back to the north-west as I was taking my wife and son home that night. I got a call three hours into the journey to tell me I had to be in for training at 9am the next day. I had no problem with us being in, the manager had to be seen as doing something, but he could have told me before I left to drive back to Bury.

I was up at 4am to get back to Scotland for training. It was madness and was the straw that broke the camel's back. I rang the Burton scout later that day to say if they were still interested in a loan move then so was I.

The deal had to be done quickly as Nigel Clough wanted me to be available for a midweek game and Davie Irons just wanted rid of me, I think!

When you are signing for a new club, for some reason the FA makes it as difficult as possible with so many forms to sign and even going from Scotland to England means international clearance is needed, which takes even longer and even more paperwork. So that evening I needed a fax machine for a few hours.

My best mate was the manager of a bookies in Sale and had to clear it with his head office first, but for a couple of hours that night instead of passing betting slips over the counter I was passing FA registration forms and contracts while on the phone to the club secretaries of both clubs.

All these deadline-day deals, during which Sky Sports reporters stand outside training grounds trying to catch a glimpse of a new £30m signing ... they should have been at the Sale branch of David Pluck bookmakers to see where the big deal was getting done courtesy of my best mate. Morton didn't end up getting rid of me completely as they were still paying nearly 40 per cent of my wages for the duration of the loan.

In the end it was probably the right decision to leave, as the manager had told me I wasn't going to be starting, and although I didn't agree with a lot of what he and his assistant said, I agreed that the travelling situation was going to affect my performances.

Deep down I was very disappointed, though, as I had been looking forward to playing at new grounds and against different opposition. Even now it is something that I think about quite often as I genuinely think I could have scored goals up in Scotland, particularly after the good season I had just had at Morecambe.

It was as though one poor performance against Livingston and a missed chance at Dundee meant Davie Irons had decided I wasn't for him as a player.

As manager that was entirely his right, of course. However, give someone a chance to show what they are capable of, not just three league starts and two substitute appearances in a league they have never played in before after missing nearly the first three weeks of pre-season training. I didn't think I was really given a fair chance up in Scotland and I would have loved to have been a success there, but I was now a Burton Albion player, albeit temporarily, and I was on the move yet again.

14

Even winning the league I never felt part of it

I HAD only signed for Burton until early January 2009 so I knew I would have to hit the ground running and impress as early as possible.

There was no problem settling into the club as I had done a day's training at the start of that pre-season and the lads were all familiar faces.

I came on briefly in a 1-0 win at Wrexham the day after I signed and then made my first appearance at the Pirelli Stadium a few days later against Weymouth in a 1-1 draw. I did well when I came on and scored a goal late on which we thought had won the game for us – only for it to be ruled out for offside. On watching it back I was a good yard onside after latching on to a Darren Stride header, and those little things were sometimes examples of the luck that deserted me.

I knew from previous experience how important it was to score early at a new club for any striker but for me, with my fragile confidence, it was absolutely imperative. Just when I thought I was off and running the linesman's poor decision stopped me in my tracks.

At Burton we trained three days a week on a Monday, Tuesday and Thursday on the site of the now new FA base at St George's

Park. The pitches there were like carpets, and although there were no buildings yet, strictly speaking a Conference team had the best training ground in the country.

There was no masterplan at training. It was relaxed and very simple and we would do similar things every day with possession practices and small-sided games. There was nothing complicated and Nigel Clough was clever like that. He rarely coached tactically, but he knew exactly what he wanted from his players.

The lads enjoyed his training and his methods, and he knew that. His ways gave the players licence to express themselves in training which they then took on to the pitch in games. He wanted to play exciting, attacking football.

At the same time, though, Clough expected the basics to be done right. He wanted his forwards to get hold of the ball, defenders to defend and midfielders to play the simple pass, and if you didn't then you had to be ready for the backlash. There was no disputing who was in charge as I found out in my first start at Rushden & Diamonds.

I played up front with Greg Pearson, who wasn't brilliant on the ball but was scoring for fun and posted a lot of important goals for Burton that season. His performances were often inconsistent but his scoring record was first-class.

I had played okay at Rushden with very little service in a poor first half, but right on the stroke of half-time Daryl Clare, who had been Burton's star striker the previous season, gave Rushden the lead.

Had he scored after 20 minutes then I don't think it would have been so bad, but because the goal came on the stroke of half-time all hell broke loose when we got back to the dressing room. I can honestly say in my entire career I've never had a bollocking like the one Clough gave me and Greg that day. He even opened the dressing room door so everyone in the ground could hear!

At the time one of Rushden's players, Andy Burgess, had a non-league column in the *Daily Mirror* on a Monday and I had to smile when he gave the incident a mention a couple of days later, saying he had never heard anything like it.

The manager destroyed me and Greg at the top of his voice for a good five minutes but as he ranted on it started to get personal, calling us every name under the sun.

I later found out that that was just his way, when the lads recounted some of the times that he'd gone at them in the past. Although I'm fairly quiet it got to a stage where I thought he was going a bit far with the insults and went to say something back, but as I opened my mouth to speak, I caught midfielder John McGrath slowly shaking his head at me and mouthing 'no' across the dressing room, so I decided I'd better let the manager get on with it.

We were both dragged off at half-time and we hadn't even been that bad. It was an interesting start to my time at Burton.

That was how Nigel Clough was, though, and on the way home on the coach he'd have his wine and cheeseboard out offering you a drink and asking how the wife and kids were. In the world of football, if you fell out with everyone you had an argument with you would never speak to anyone again. I always viewed that as part and parcel of the game. He was just a manager whose ways I would have to get used to.

After the Rushden defeat, I was on the bench and getting half an hour in most matches. The team was hovering around the top three and there was genuine optimism that this could be the year Burton made it into the Football League for the first time. That would be a remarkable achievement considering Burton's part-time status and the presence of other clubs with much bigger budgets who already had many years of Football League experience.

That group included Oxford United, who beat us 2-1 in October, when I had a really good half-hour after coming on and playing on the right-hand side of midfield in an old-fashioned 4-4-2 formation.

The performance helped me get my first start in a month on 1 November, at home to Ebbsfleet, at the start of an incredible record-breaking winning run that went a long way to helping the club win promotion.

I started on the right again and made the second goal for Keith Gilroy on a day when I won my one man of the match award for Burton. I then started the next six matches, all wide on the right, and we won all six.

I wasn't doing anything spectacular I but was helping the team to keep chalking up wins, and the closest I came to a goal was an effort against the foot of the post at Forest Green.

I missed both games over the Christmas period when Josh was in hospital with suspected meningitis in what was a scary time for us. Nigel Clough and all the staff at the club were very supportive of us as a family, which meant a lot.

My return to the squad was on New Year's Day at York City and I wasn't expecting to play for two reasons. Firstly, I had missed the last two matches while Josh was ill and we had won both of them to take our winning run to ten, and secondly only a week earlier Clough had told me that my loan spell was unlikely to be extended. The York game was looking like being my last for the club before I headed back up to Scotland for the rest of the season.

The manager spoke to me on the pitch at Bootham Crescent and told me most players not having their loan extended wouldn't play, 'but we have that trust in you to do a job for us'.

Those words meant a lot to me and we won 3-1 to take our run to 33 points out of a possible 33. I had my best game in a Burton shirt by a mile. As I left the pitch in the 86th minute the manager told me I had given him a 'proper performance'.

After the game I spoke with 'Mr Burton', physio Matt Brown, who told me there was no way the manager would send me back up to Scotland after a performance like that, and a couple of days later my loan was extended until the end of the season which effectively saw my Morton career come to an end.

There was major upheaval at Burton , though, early in January as Clough left to take over at Championship side Derby County.

It was a massive moment for the club with Clough having been the manager for so many years and many of the players were very disappointed about his departure.

He came across as a father figure to some of the players and whoever was coming in to replace him would have massive shoes to fill. His training was so simple and enjoyable, and the players loved the intensity of the possession and small-sided games.

Oh, and the cricket! When the weather prevented us from training outside we would go to an indoor training centre in Derby and before playing five-a-side we would have an hour playing cricket. The manager was a proper player. If I thought Clough had been angry that day at Rushden & Diamonds, it was nothing compared to how angry he became if someone on his team dropped a catch or didn't dive full-length to stop a boundary. He would be fuming!

I didn't get much praise from him that season for my football, but after hitting a straight drive back past the bowler for four I got the shout of, 'Now that's a proper cricket shot!' And that would do for me.

Clough was replaced by former England player Roy McFarland and the difference between the two in terms of style was chalk and cheese. The training went from lively, intense small-sided games to long, drawn-out sessions of team shape based on who we were playing that week. With Clough in charge the emphasis had always been on us not the opposition but the new training sessions became boring for a group of players who were used to the exact opposite.

When new managers come in there are always changes, and players will embrace them if they think they are going to make things better, but if you're almost 20 points clear at the top of the league it's obvious there is not much that needs altering. Roy worked in a totally different way to the previous manager, however, and it didn't really benefit the team.

We did win his first game in charge, 1-0 at Grays Athletic, which gave us a record 12 consecutive victories, but I sat on the bench for 90 minutes and it was a sign of things to come. Out of that run I had started eight games and I know I played my part in helping the team achieve their end goal come the end of the season.

Once Clough had left, the season became a write-off for me. The new manager just didn't fancy me as a player, and I didn't get a look-in. Most matchdays saw me either sat on the bench or in the stand for 90 minutes and in the last three months I made just a handful of substitute appearances as we just about held on to top spot in the league.

We knew other teams would also go on good runs, but we went on a couple of bad ones at the same time as them and were so inconsistent. McFarland was almost too nice to the players. Clough knew the players inside out and would have known the minute they needed a bollocking to get the season back on track, but we just drifted and were hoping we would get over the line as the pressure built.

Out of the last six games we lost five and went in to three of them knowing a win meant we were champions. Each time, though, we lost and going into the last match, at Torquay United, there was a real possibility we could blow it. We went into that final week of the season knowing that a point would see the club promoted into the Football League. If we lost, then our only challengers, Cambridge United, would have to beat strugglers Altrincham by four goals to overtake us at the top of the table.

It was a strange week and the longer it went on the more the pressure seemed to be building, but we knew even a stumble over the line would be enough.

The match was on the Sunday with all the games kicking off at the same time, but rather than train at Burton the day before as normal, we did something I had never seen before in football. The chairman arranged for us to go and train at Derby County with the previous manager!

After Roy McFarland had taken his normal team-shape session, Nigel Clough took the lads for some small-sided games and the session was fizzing again, with him getting into the boys and creating an intensity.

It was unheard of for the old manager to take the session before the biggest game of the season, while our current manager watched from the sidelines. I think it showed how worried those at the top were of the team missing out on the promotion that the club deserved.

The game at Torquay, with Clough watching from the stands, didn't go to plan and despite an early Marc Goodfellow goal giving us the lead, we lost 2-1. I was a sub, and we were kept well informed of the score at Cambridge – and when their match finished goalless, we were promoted regardless of our defeat.

After the winning run we had been on earlier in the season we were deservedly crowned champions as Burton became a Football League club for the first time in their history. There were some emotional scenes on the pitch at the final whistle and the many people, who had worked wonders for the club for many years deserved to share in the happiness that the players had earned.

My celebrations were a bit more muted. Yes, I was pleased that I had played a part in the promotion, especially during that winning run, but I hadn't started a league game in the last four months and was nothing more than a bit-part player. I was delighted for the players who played every week, and a few of them had been on a long journey over the years with the club, but it wasn't a season that I could look back on with any real personal satisfaction and I don't think I have ever looked at the winners' medal I received after the game.

I was to get my own 'winners' medal' soon after the season finished, however, when Wendy gave birth to our second child, Olivia. She was more important than any promotion.

15

It was a club I wasn't sad to leave

I WOULD be 31 just a few months into the new season and it looked likely I would now be dropping into non-league football on a permanent basis.

The manager from my first spell at Bury – and the one I had enjoyed working with the most – Andy Preece had taken over at Conference North club Northwich Victoria. Having had a good working and personal relationship with him I decided to sign for him while working towards my coaching badges as I looked at a life after playing.

It was a really strange set-up from the start. Northwich had been relegated from the Conference in the same season that Burton had been champions and they were also in administration, and hardly anything about the club felt right. Really, though, I had gone to play for Preecey as opposed to Northwich.

There were about eight players who were classed as 'full time', which meant we trained two mornings a week and then also two evenings a week with the players who worked during the day, and it just didn't work with such a small number of full-time players. The training during the day only lasted until October as by then we weren't getting paid on time, or the full amount we were due.

There were some great lads at the club. My former Morecambe team-mate Simon Grand was captain and Mike Aspin, Danny

Meadowcroft, Lee Elam, Jon D'Laryea and goalkeepers James Spencer and Curtis Aspden had all played in higher leagues. They, like the manager and his assistant Andy 'Jock' Morrison, all wanted things done right and as professional as possible, but most things were out of their hands.

I struggled with the part-time mentality of some players in the squad, but it wasn't their fault. They had never been full time and they worked during the day, so coming to play football was a release for them and a way to earn a bit more money, whereas football had taken over my life completely for at least the last 13 years.

I pushed myself too hard in pre-season and in the early matches for Northwich and pulled my hamstring badly in just the third game of the season. So I was already on the sidelines for six weeks.

During that time the money situation at the club began to get worse and Preecey would be fighting fires, telling the players everything would be fine in a few weeks.

Some weeks our wages were a lot less than we had agreed, and other weeks they weren't there at all. We were often paid by a cheque which would bounce, or you would end up paying an international clearance fee as they were registered to a bank in a far-flung corner of the world.

It wasn't a situation I could get my head round and I've no idea why non-league chairmen in particular promise wages that they simply can't pay and then bale out of the club a few months later.

There wasn't much that was positive to talk about during the season other than our FA Cup run. After beating a team much lower down the pyramid we were drawn against FC United, and as a big Liverpool supporter and former player I grew to love playing against them as they would always take a massive following of Manchester United fans everywhere that they went.

You had to respect how they built a new club from scratch in protest at how the Old Trafford club was being run, and this was the closest any of us were going to get to playing Manchester United. Every game became a cup final for them with the atmosphere that their fans created.

There were more FC United supporters than Northwich fans as we beat them 3-0 at home and I made the third goal as I went clean through on goal and squared the ball to Wayne Riley for a simple tap-in. The momentum of my run took me off the pitch behind the goal where a few polite Mancunians thought they would remind me of my Scouse background and put a few words alongside it too.

I didn't engage in too many pleasantries with them but I did give them a quick reminder with a hand signal that Liverpool had won five European Cups, along with my nicest smile. There was nearly a riot in the far corner of the Victoria Stadium, but it was nice to play in a game with a bit of an atmosphere again and FC United fans always guaranteed that.

I had timed my return from my hamstring injury well and came on as a sub that day. I then started at Stafford Rangers where I scored my first Northwich goal in a 2-2 draw, the week before we were due to play against League 1 side Charlton Athletic in the FA Cup.

I knew Preecey would want to play me against Charlton for my experience and I was looking forward to playing opposition from a much higher level in a game that was to be televised live.

We had a real belief that we could cause Charlton problems so the manager and Jock worked hard at drilling the players in terms of their tactical focus and exactly where they wanted us in certain situations. Jock's attention to detail on certain things was second to none and I learnt a lot from him at Northwich.

One thing that we worked unbelievably hard on was set-pieces. We had great delivery and players who would attack the ball. The centre-half pairing of Nat Kerr and 6ft 6in Matt Bailey was a massive threat and midfielder Michael O'Connor would have headed bricks if they were thrown into the box.

An early photo with my brother David. A mish-mash of kits. Crystal Palace for him. I have no idea what shorts I'm wearing but the Liver bird is on my chest from an early age.

The yellow and green of Penketh United, my first junior team in Warrington

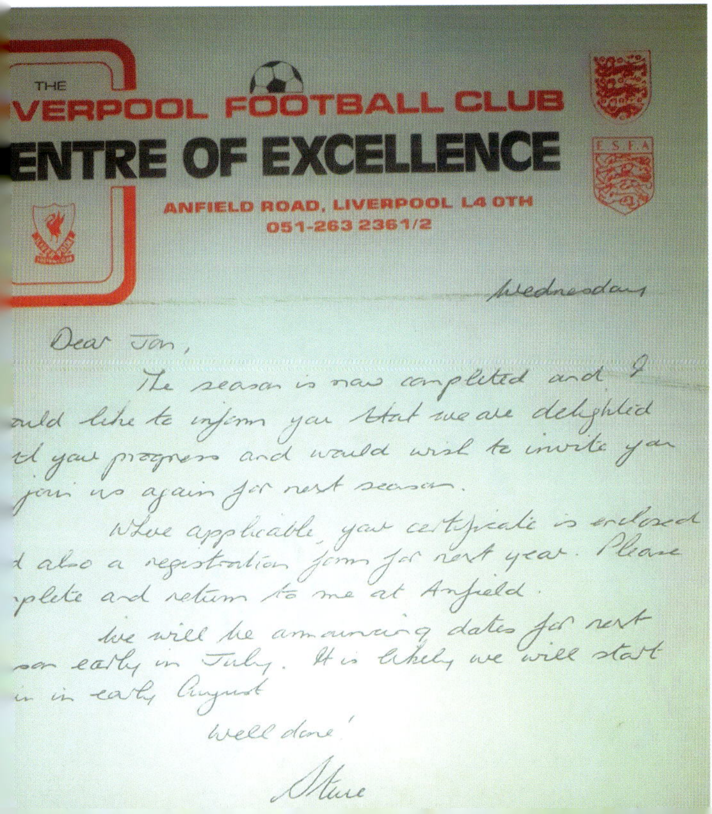

THE
VERPOOL FOOTBALL CLUB
ENTRE OF EXCELLENCE
ANFIELD ROAD, LIVERPOOL L4 0TH
051-263 2361/2

Wednesday

Dear Jon,

The season is now completed and I
uld like to inform you that we are delighted
d your progress and would wish to invite you
join us again for next season.

Where applicable, your certificate is enclosed
d also a registration form for next year. Please
plete and return to me at Anfield.

We will be announcing dates for next
son early in July. It is likely we will start
in in early August

Well done!

Steve

The no-frills way in which all the boys at Liverpool were told we were being retained for the following season. A letter from Steve Heighway inviting us to return. This was at the end of my first season in 1989.

The 1996 FA Youth Cup winning team. There were some crazy characters and fantastic footballers in this team. A special group of players.

21 September 1999 was the moment I had waited for since I was a boy as I made my first team debut for Liverpool at Anfield against Hull City in the League Cup.

Playing for Liverpool reserves in the mini derby at Anfield against Everton in April 2000.

Playing for Sheffield United away at Wolverhampton Wanderers in September 2000.

My final game for Liverpool at a near deserted Villa Park for the reserves.

A pre-season game for Bury against Manchester United in 2001.

Bolton 0-1 Bury

Worthington Cup

Bury's inspirational captain Jon Newby provided the impetus as Bolton were knocked out of the Worthington Cup.

Bolton manager Sam Allardyce's gamble in fielding a second-string side for this second round match backfired badly.

Newby personified his side's desire.

The former Liverpool striker has been the target of several bigger and richer clubs - including West Brom in the summer, but he has elected to stay at Bury.

It was Newby who fired in a cross which was bundled into his own net by Bernard Mendy under pressure from Colin Woodthorpe.

Allardyce's restructured side ensured three debuts, two of which ended in disappointment.

Chris Armstrong was substituted after 53 minutes, while Turkish midfielder Akin Bulent lasted 11 minutes longer but also left the field early - sent off for up two cautions.

Three minutes after the break Bury achieved the reward for their first-half exertions by taking the lead.

Not surprisingly it was Newby at the heart of the move, the centre-forward bursting down the right, forcing his way into the box and firing in a low cross which ended up in the net.

Mendy looked sheepish and it was Newby rather than Woodthorpe who accepted the congratulations of his team-mates.

Another penetrating run by Newby created more havoc in the Bolton defence but when he found Terry Dunfield the Canadian fired too high.

Kevin Nolan came off the bench for Bolton and almost had an immediate impact forcing Glynn Garner into a sprawling stop.

Nolan and Dean Holdsworth then interchanged passes twice to split open Bury's defence but Nolan stumbled at the crucial moment and Garner was able to gather.

The home side piled on the pressure in six minutes of injury time, but Chris Billy nearly added a second for Bury on the break, shooting over from near the penalty spot.

The manager who got the best out of me. Congratulating Andy Preece after we knocked Stoke City out of the League Cup at Gigg Lane in 2002.

The BBC match report as Bury beat local rivals Bolton Wanderers in the League Cup.

The League Cup run came to an end in a 3-1 defeat against Premier League side Fulham where I grabbed a last-minute goal.

Moaning at Mark Clattenburg during the 2002/03 season. Whatever he had done I finally forgave him when he awarded Liverpool three penalties at Old Trafford in 2014!

Chasing a lost cause for York City in a League 2 game against Cheltenham Town in 2004.

Equalising for Bury away at Boston in a League 2 game in 2005 as we came back from 2-0 down to grab a point.

A battle with my old team-mate Danny Swailes in a game for Bury against Macclesfield Town in 2005

Wrexham took Birmingham City to extra time in a cup tie in 2006 but we were eventually beaten 4-1.

Celebrations as Morecambe beat Wolves 3-1 in a League Cup tie at Molineux in 2007.

Scoring on my Scottish League debut for Morton away at Clyde in 2008

In action for Northwich Victoria during the FA Cup run in 2009 which saw us knock out Charlton Athletic.

What a moment! The goal that sent Colwyn Bay to the highest league in their history as we beat FC United in the play-off final.

In action for Warrington Town away at Salford City in 2013.

(Below, left): My family – wife Wendy, daughter Olivia and son Josh.

(Below, right): Never be ashamed of a scar. My ICD is clearly visible under my skin, but it is a necessity that helps to save my life when I need it to and is now part and parcel of my life.

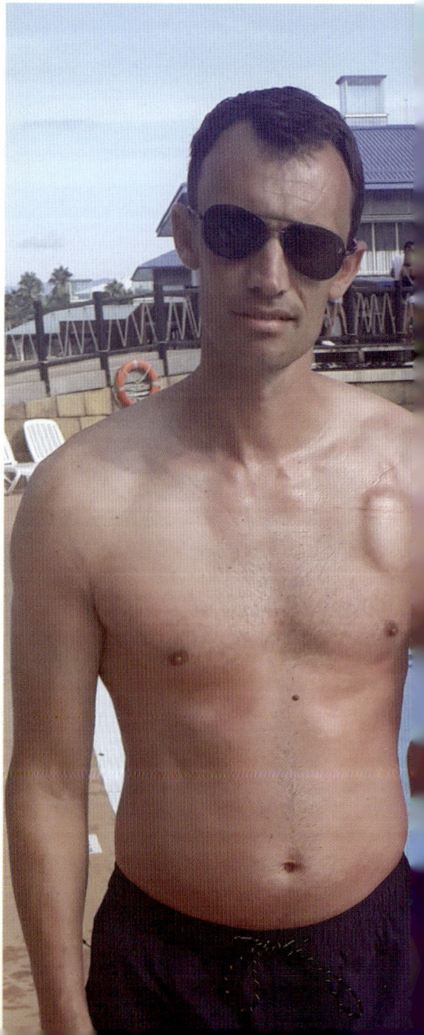

We also had Ian 'Spud' Herring who could throw the ball as far as Dave Challinor could back in his Tranmere days, and we almost played to get as many throw-ins as we could in the final third.

On a bad day Spud could throw the ball with pace to the front post. On a good day he would hit the penalty spot, and this was one of his very good days. We bombarded Charlton with an aerial threat and they were hanging on at times. It was a proper old-fashioned cup tie full of goalmouth scrambles and incident.

The build-up to the game, with the cameras following us, created a bit of drama and excitement for the fans and it was great to carry my son Josh out on to the pitch as mascot before the match got under way.

Charlton had a full-strength team including Darren Randolph in goal, Christian Dailly at the back, a young Jonjo Shelvey in midfield and Izale Mcleod up front. On the day we just wanted it more and young substitute Wayne Riley poked a loose ball home with ten minutes to go. To a man we were magnificent and deserved to go through to the next round.

That cup run apparently generated in the region of £300,000 for Northwich and we thought that with all the prize money, television revenue, gate receipts and sponsorship that we might at least get paid on time that month, but no such luck with the tax man taking most of the money to stop the club from being closed down. Not even so much as a £50 bonus came the way of the players, even though we were again televised in the next round as we faced more league opposition in Lincoln City, who beat us 3-1 at the Victoria Stadium.

I finished the season with another goal in a win against Stalybridge Celtic, but nearly all the players left at the end of the campaign. We were still chasing weeks of wages owed to us throughout the following months, and we didn't see much of that either.

I remember that summer I saw the Northwich chairman pull on to the M6 as I was on my way to play for my new club

Colwyn Bay at Witton Albion, whose ground was literally next to Northwich's. He still owed me four weeks' wages, so I rang him.

'All right chairman, I'm not far from the ground so I'll come and pick up that money you owe me,' I said.

'I'm not in the country, Newbs. It's at the ground waiting for you though,' was his reply as the line went dead. I could only shake my head in disbelief.

I did nip into the ground but there was no money, as expected. To be fair to Preecey he did, in the end, get us some of the money we were owed even though we had left the club.

At one stage during the season the groundsman had not been paid for so long that we players, would all put at least £10 into an envelope for him every few weeks so at least he had some money coming in.

I felt sorry for the supporters that one of the most famous non-league clubs in the country was in such a mess, with a chairman who felt he was doing both the players and ground staff a favour by paying us every so often.

However, it was off to pastures new in what would be one of the most enjoyable seasons I ever had.

16

Favourites to go down

I WAS in bed late one night when my former Bury team-mate Dave Challinor messaged me telling me that he and another old mate, Colin Woodthorpe, were the new management team at Evo-Stik Northern Premier League team Colwyn Bay and asked me if I fancied joining them. With those two at the helm, men I both liked and respected, the opportunity really appealed to me.

Chall wanted a mix of youth and experience to get the right balance on the pitch. In me, Damian Allen and Fraser McLachlan we had plenty of Football League experience and in Danny Meadowcroft, Chris Sanna and Luke Denson we had a lot of non-league knowhow.

Colwyn Bay had been promoted through the play-offs in the previous season and, despite the fact that inside the club we knew we had a decent, hard-working squad ready for the year ahead, as we travelled to our opening day match at North Ferriby United near Hull, the *Non-League Paper* had us down as rank outsiders to win the league and certain favourites to be relegated.

North Ferriby had a nice little ground in the shadows of the Humber Bridge. It was a five-hour drive away from the North Wales coast of Colwyn Bay, but even so we took a few supporters who travelled with us on the team bus. Supporters at the front, players at the back, the perfect arrangement when things are going well, but it would be interesting to see how it worked after a 5-0 away defeat.

It was a good afternoon to be on the same bus as the fans as, in glorious sunshine, we won 3-1 to get the season off to the perfect start and I scored twice on my debut. The relegation favourites were off and running.

We trained twice a week, usually in Chester so that we weren't travelling all the way to North Wales. We had an unbelievable team spirit and I travelled in with four lads who lived in Manchester.

Our car school consisted of Danny Meadowcroft, who had a lot of experience from his days at Stockport County and Morecambe and had an encyclopaedic knowledge of non-league football. He was a funny lad with some of the worst yet best jokes you'd ever hear and if you mentioned a player's name, Meads would always have a story about them. He must have played with about 5,000 players in his career. He knew everyone.

Next up was Damien Allen, who would be our captain that season. Damo should have been playing higher but had fallen out of love with the game a bit.

Then there was Fraser McLachlan who, like Damo, had been a team-mate of mine at Morecambe. He was an excellent footballer and very underrated. He was also by far the most laid-back player I've ever played with. He did everything at his own pace. He would get screamed at by the manager to do things quicker, but he would tell Chall to calm down with a puzzled look on his face and still seem to have loads of time on the ball! He was our penalty taker and used to wait for the keeper to dive then roll the ball the other way so slowly that it barely crossed the line. But he never missed.

Last, but not least, was Mike 'Leggy' Lea who earned his nickname when a receptionist at a hotel continually called him Mr Leg. Mike had been a youth player at Manchester United and then had a taste of football abroad with Antwerp in Belgium and was another that could have played much higher in my opinion.

The five of us got on brilliantly and kept each other going on the long drives.

There were a few other car schools in the squad and there used to be a little battle as to which one brought the most worth to the team. Living the furthest away and getting stuck in traffic, we often got to games bang on the meeting time and would breeze in claiming the 'real players' had arrived.

'Don't worry boys,' we'd say. 'Everything's all right now, they'll be 350 here this afternoon now we've turned up. We've just put another 100 on the gate.'

Everything was said tongue in cheek and in good spirit, and it created a brilliant atmosphere among us all. If we won on an away trip one of the directors would give the lads some money for a few drinks at the first off licence on the way home, which would make for a great journey back, although we were occasionally a man down when one of the lads would find himself bundled in the storage compartment of the coach and end up doing a few miles in the dark! It sounds daft, but things like that helped make us successful that season. In some games we were under unbelievable pressure, but the lads would have gone to war for each other that year to get results.

The biggest club and the favourites to win the league were FC Halifax Town. They had the largest fanbase having been formed from the ashes of a former Football League club and that gave them the biggest budget.

Having the most resources at that level spoke volumes as they could go and sign the best players. Only the league winners would get automatic promotion, with the four teams below qualifying for the play-offs, and the winner of that final would join the champions in Conference North.

That season we went to Halifax in just the fourth game, drawing 1-1 and were more than a match for them.

Having the management team of Chall and Col, with such a vast amount of experience, helped us no end. Chall knew the club, having been a player at Llanelian Road the season before he became manager, but the two of them ran Colwyn Bay as they would have done if it was a league club, and I don't think we would have had the same success if we'd had a 'non-league' manager in charge. They knew when to have a laugh with the lads, when to get serious and when to give us a bollocking.

We played three up front and I always played on the left. The personnel alongside me changed a fair bit, but in the early stages Karl Noon would be the central striker and he was a good player. Noony wasn't the tallest but his hold-up play was good, and he was clever and inventive, so we linked up well.

We were inconsistent in the first third of the season, but we were always in and around the top eight. It was an enjoyable team to play in and, after my double on the opening day, I got further goals at Kendal, Whitby and Stocksbridge where we won with a certain Jamie Vardy in the opposition line-up.

I also scored at home against Bradford Park Avenue, Burscough and a late winning penalty against Buxton. We had a slight blip over the Christmas period when losing 4-0 and 3-0 in successive games, but we were boosted by the return of our former striker Rob Hopley. Hops played as the central striker with me and Noony either side and it kicked us on to another level.

My favourite games of the season were always against FC United. As they had done the previous season when I was with Northwich, their fans created an atmosphere, and with my Liverpool connections I always seemed to be in the firing line for a fair bit of stick.

I loved it, even more so as in three out of the four games we played against them that season I scored important goals. We beat them 3-1 at home before Christmas where I scored to put us 2-1 up, and again I celebrated with a trademark five European Cup salute which always seemed to anger the Mancunians.

We had a good record on the road that season, too, and defensively we soaked up so much pressure and would then hit teams on the counter attack. We won 4-1 at Bradford PA where I scored once, and Hops got a terrific hat-trick, but we were the masters of going away for a smash-and-grab 1-0 victory after being under the cosh.

One of these games was at my old stomping ground, Gigg Lane, where FC United played, and again I got the winner. It felt nice to go 'home' and it had been a while since Newby had got the winner at Gigg Lane.

February saw a really influential player join us as we signed pacy winger Jimmy McCarthy. He was full of tricks and had a Challinor-style long throw which we used to our advantage. He was brilliant for us in the last three months of the season.

It was during these months that assistant manager Colin Woodthorpe became resident DJ in the dressing rooms after games, blasting out Queen's 'Another One Bites the Dust' after every victory with all the lads singing along.

I was surprised that an opposition team didn't kick our dressing room door through on hearing that particular song, and a few managers I had played for definitely would have done. But it added to the togetherness that we already had in the squad.

With Halifax way out in front and more or less champions already, we were left to fight it out for a play-off place and had a good run-in, apart from one poor display at home to Stocksbridge when we lost 4-3. Our regular centre-half Danny Meadowcroft rang in sick on the morning only to ring us again later from Wembley singing Manchester City songs as he celebrated their FA Cup semi-final win. That was the life of a non-league player!

We were brilliant in the last 12 games and kept eight clean sheets, winning nine times with the centre-back pairing of Meadowcroft and big Joe McMahon in imperious form. With two games to go we won 1-0 at Hucknall Town, where I scored the winner early in the second half, to secure our play-off place as we finished runners-up behind Halifax.

The play-offs were all one-off ties and as we had finished second it meant we would be at home in the semi-final and also the final should we progress.

In our semi-final against North Ferriby they were, in truth, probably the better footballing side, but we knew how to win and we were good at it.

Rob Hopley gave us the lead early in the game and Jimmy McCarthy scored the second on the stroke of half-time with an extremely brave header where he almost got his head punched off by the goalkeeper. In the same move that led to Jimmy's goal, as I had played the ball wide, I had collided with a defender, smashing my head on his knee, and was knocked out by the halfway line. The pitch resembled a bit of a battleground with players crowding round the both of us and physios rushing here there and everywhere. We both came round but had to be taken off and it was a rejigged team for the second half.

I was taken to the local hospital by one of the club directors, Mark Williams, to have my head glued as quickly as possible so I could have the best chance of playing in the final, but the journey back to the ground was an anxious one as I was glued to a mobile phone getting commentary off one of the fans to make sure we were still in front.

We saw the game out winning 2-0 and would play FC United in the final, but with Jimmy Mac almost certainly out and me doubtful the pressure was starting to grow with only three days until the big showdown.

It was on the first Bank Holiday Monday in May and the weekend seemed to be the longest one of my life. I was desperate to get on with things. I always used to get nervous before any match, but this was different.

It was fear, not of the occasion approaching or not playing well, but of losing and how I would feel if we were to be beaten. It was different to anything I had felt before in football. We had been written off. I had been written off and now we were 90 minutes away from 'the relegation certainties' winning promotion. Getting beat was simply unthinkable.

The ground would be full. All 2,500 tickets had been sold and about 2,000 of those fans would be from FC United. There was also a field next to the ground on a slope and it was a better view than actually being inside, so there were another 1,000 expected there.

The one thing that would help us was our team spirit. It was as good as I've known in my career; we knew we would fight for each other. Even the lads who didn't start every week – such as Lee Davey, Alex Titchener and Danny Grannon – brought so much over the course of the season. I think our team spirit alone had gained us ten points at least with our willingness to battle and help do each other's jobs on the pitch.

On the day itself I was fit to play. There was no chance I wouldn't be, but Jimmy McCarthy didn't make it. He still couldn't open his eye so it would have been impossible for him, and he would be a big miss.

The game was scrappy and there wasn't much quality. It was very hot on the day. The pitch was rock-hard, and every second touch was trying to get your first touch under control from the bobbles. It was the type of pitch footballers hate to play on.

FC United put us under a real spell of pressure on the hour, backed by their vocal support, and our keeper Chris Sanna made a couple of key saves to keep the score level.

The one real piece of quality in the game saw Damien Allen lift a perfectly weighted pass over the two FC United centre-backs and I made a diagonal run from the left. My first touch took me in to the penalty area and I had a quick glance to see if I could give anyone a tap-in, but on realising I was on my own I slotted the ball past the keeper to give us the lead with just under 20 minutes left.

Jon Newby through on goal against FC United that season only seemed to end in one outcome. It was one of the best feelings I've had in football – the very best coming when the final whistle went.

The celebration that followed the goal made me laugh. I once again had my hand up showing off Liverpool's five European Cups, but because of the magnitude of the game this time I had an Everton supporter and a Manchester City supporter jumping all over me displaying the exact same celebration to those FC United fans. Who says followers of all these other clubs hate Liverpool?

When the final whistle blew the emotion was one of absolute euphoria. For the initial 20 seconds or so it was the best feeling I had ever had in the game. I suppose it was the same as players feel when they win massive competitions. The Agüero moment in 2012, the Origi Champions League Final goal in 2019, Dudek's 2005 penalty save. This was our moment, our Champions League Final, and even though it was Colwyn Bay and not Manchester City or Liverpool, if I could have bottled the feeling I had at that moment and drunk it in every so often I absolutely would have done.

I don't remember too much of what happened after the game. It was all a bit of a blur, but for the relegation favourites to gain promotion to Conference North, the highest status in the club's history, was a great achievement no matter what the level was.

It had been such an enjoyable and satisfying season and I was made up for Chall and Col, who I had known for many years and who were my mates as much as my manager and coach.

There were others at the club who did so much, and seeing their local team win in front of a packed stadium would have meant so much to them. Roger Skinner, who was one of the directors who the lads got on great with – especially after he'd had about eight cans of lager on the way home from an away trip – had tears in his eyes at the end of the game. There was Bill Murray, the treasurer, who was valued so much at the club; Sheila and Tommy who volunteered in the club shop every week; Tim Channon who did a fantastic job reporting and writing on each and every game home and away for years; Trefor Jones who ran the supporters' away coach travel; and groundsman Elfed Morris, who kept the pitch in great condition. The joy that season brought to those people was something they would remember forever.

I finished as top scorer with 14 goals, although we still had two games to play in the North Wales Cup, where I scored twice as we won the semi-final and added another one in the final. We ended the season in style. The lads joked that there would be a statue of me built somewhere in the area, and still to this day I can't believe I didn't at least get the Colwyn Bay pier renamed after me for a week or so!

Club officials even decided there would be an open-top bus parade through the town on the night of the end-of-season presentation awards. We thought they were joking at first. When we realised that they weren't, we tried as players to convince them that it wasn't a good idea! It was no fun freezing to death in pouring rain on the top deck of that bus with the wind coming in off the sea and only about 50 fans on the route through the town giving us a wave.

One local pensioner even stuck his hand out trying to stop the bus thinking it was the number 12 to Rhyl!

But for once it was a relaxing, satisfying summer break and this time a season that I could look back on with a huge amount of satisfaction.

17

Do you want the job?

THE FOLLOWING season, 2011/12, started as the previous one had ended. With us winning.

We went away to Bishop's Stortford, who despite being only 40 miles outside London were in the Conference North. I captained the side for the first time and we won 2-0.

During the summer there had been a change in the day-to-day running of the club with owner and chairman Geoff Cartwright and his son Darren leaving. They were two down-to-earth people who made it their business to get to know the players and they were missed by the lads. Fellow director Bob Paton took over the immediate running of matters.

We had managed to keep the majority of the squad together despite Chall letting a few players go, thinking that the step up to the sixth tier of English football might be too much for them.

We also signed a couple of good players in John McKenna, a ball-winning midfielder, and Liverpool lad Danny Lloyd, who was a lively winger with a great work ethic. They would both be good additions who also fitted well into the dressing room. Chall would later bring in experienced striker Lee McEvilly, who had been a former team-mate of mine at Wrexham.

After the good opening-day result we lost at home to Hyde but then drew 1-1 away at Halifax where I gave us the lead from the penalty spot, only for a lively Jamie Vardy to earn a point for the Shaymen with a stunning strike. Although we were picking up points, it was obvious that life would be much tougher for the team at this level.

We had further victories at home to Workington Town, where I scored a late winner, and away at Gloucester City, who played at nearby Football League side Cheltenham Town's ground after theirs had been damaged by floods. On a good surface we played some great football and again I scored late on, after good work from Karl Noon, for my third goal of the season.

Our next six games, however, brought just five points, including a good 2-2 draw away at former Football League club Boston United. On the long trip home there was no sign of what was to come that week.

On the Wednesday night we had a local cup tie at home but before it, Col asked to see me and told me that both him and Chall would be leaving the club. It was a massive shock. They were dropping two divisions to take over at AFC Fylde. It was a brave move by them, but the right one as Fylde were a club with a lot of ambition and had the money to see it through.

Col also told me that the chairman, Bob Paton, was going to ask me to take over the manager's role on a temporary basis, which was an even bigger shock.

I can't remember anything about the game that night other than coming off after an hour and the chairman walking round to the dugout as I was subbed to ask if he could have a word. Bob and the club secretary Grant McIndoe took me into the clubhouse and very briefly told me that Chall and Col were leaving and that they had been watching how I was about the club for some time, and they saw me as the right person to take over the manager's role.

'Do you want the job?' the chairman asked.

'Yes,' I replied without hesitation. We shook hands there and then. That was it. Nothing more. There was no money or contracts discussed. I saw it as an opportunity, and on 2 November 2011 I was appointed player-manager of Colwyn Bay.

Nothing was broken at the club, so I didn't envisage any major changes to fix anything. I wanted everything to run as it had been with me simply putting my own stamp and personality on things.

My first game in charge was a tough one, with a long trip to Blyth Spartans in the north-east. At that time I had no assistant manager, and the physio was working nights so couldn't travel. It was like a Sunday league game in the sixth tier of English football.

I didn't pick myself as there was so much going on and I named myself as one of the subs instead.

It is a totally different feeling being a manager. Everything is your responsibility and you feel it. Whether it's the Premier League or Conference North there is pressure and management isn't really something you enjoy, you just live it. There is a lot more planning, too.

As a player you prepare for yourself and what will get the best out of you. As a manager you have to get the best out of everyone. There are tactics to plan, set-piece charts to write out and the tone and content of the team talk to decide on. And mentally you never stop thinking. As a player you almost just turn up and play.

We got off to the worst possible start as Leggy scored an own goal inside the first three minutes. With nobody else on the bench that day, apart from the subs, there wasn't even anyone to bounce ideas off.

Noony equalised before half-time, but we found ourselves 2-1 down going into the last ten minutes and it looked as though my first game in charge would end in defeat. But if you can't beat them join them, as the saying goes, and I threw myself on with just six minutes left. Deep into injury time Lee McEvilly flicked on a long ball and I managed to poke it past the goalkeeper from about ten yards out for a last-gasp equaliser.

The goal was celebrated by us all as though we had just scored in the World Cup Final. It's easy this management lark. If the team are struggling just put yourself on and rescue the lads! It was some start to life as a manager.

The next week was another interesting one as captain Damian Allen was sold to Bangor City. The deal was in the pipeline before I took over. Damo would be a big loss to us but at least there was a transfer fee involved – a small amount of cash and a few stand seats! Bangor had recently moved to a new ground and as part of the deal Colwyn Bay got some stand seats as there were some early plans to improve our ground at some stage.

I also had to bring in an assistant manager to help me. As a club we were punching well above our weight in Conference North, in terms of budgets and the structure of the club, and bringing in an assistant would be a tall order with the money I had available to pay someone – just £110.

My weekly budget was £2,900 and with that I had to pay the 16 players that were in the matchday squad, sometimes 17 if you picked a different player on a Tuesday who hadn't been in the squad on the Saturday, and I also had to pay myself, the assistant and the physio. That was 19 or 20 people each week.

Apart from Vauxhall Motors there wasn't a team with a smaller budget than that and some teams had six times as much to pay their players. That was one of the reasons that Chall had decided to go to Fylde. He didn't see a future in which the club would be able to compete with that budget and only 350 people coming through the turnstiles every week. I simply had to make the best of it.

I wanted my assistant to be someone who had been in the game for a while, someone with experience and who was a lively character that the boys would take to. Anthony Sheehan, who had been at the club the season before, immediately sprung to mind, but he wanted to focus on playing and instead I brought in my former Bury team-mate Stuart Barlow who ticked all those boxes and wanted to get back into football. I was hoping for Stu's natural enthusiasm to rub off on the players when we needed it to.

His debut in his new role was my first home game in charge, against Gainsborough Trinity. I started myself and although we found ourselves 1-0 down at half-time, we were excellent in the second half and goals from Lee Mc, who bullied the opposition back four, and a stunner from Karl Noon gave me my first three points as manager. It was a feeling of relief rather than joy.

My first defeat came the following week, however, at top-of-the-table Hyde. It was a controversial loss, but every one as a manager would hurt.

We then drew with big-spending Halifax, 0-0 in the FA Trophy, but went away and beat them 2-1 in the replay.

Cup games became massively important because of the prize money involved. Winning that replay earned us £4,000 and that was big money to a club like Colwyn Bay. We would never be in a position to buy a player and most of those I did bring in were youngsters on loan from League 2 or Conference National clubs, or players from non-league who had impressed me and had the experience of this level. Winning in cups and earning prize money always gave me leverage with the chairman if I occasionally needed an extra £100 in the budget.

The one thing that became apparent very quickly with this job was that it was non-stop. It was a full-time job on not even part-time money because I had to do everything myself. There was no backroom staff of ten people like Alex Ferguson would have had, so he could delegate and concentrate on the things he needed to do. I had an assistant manager and a physio, both of whom worked night shifts. At times I would have so much to organise in terms of going to meet players at motorway services to sign forms, calculating the weekly budgets, booking and viewing training venues that the football side of things in terms of planning training and tactics almost became secondary.

At one stage I even took a call from the police as one of the lads had spent a night in the cells and had given them my name as his one call. I could think of better people to ring than me in that situation!

My life wasn't my own, even in charge of a Conference North team. It took over everything, as football always did for me, and no doubt my wife and children suffered because of it as I was a nightmare to be around – especially if we had lost or weren't on a good run.

I had always found it hard to relax as a player, but as a manager I just couldn't switch off at all. I couldn't find a time where I wasn't thinking about the next game or the next signing, as I had been able to do as a player. I was putting too much pressure on myself to do the job exactly as I wanted.

What I needed was a Hughie McAuley, a Dave Shannon or a Billy Ayre telling me on a matchday to go and play while they took charge of everything for those two hours, but I took my manager's head on to the pitch more than I took my player's head, as the budget didn't allow me to have exactly what I wanted alongside me.

It wasn't to say Stuart Barlow didn't do a good job, because I felt he brought what I expected he would bring to the club, but I think we both needed someone who had seen even far more than we had at that stage of our managerial roles.

As much as I could be down when we lost, I would still allow myself an hour or so of enjoyment when we won before thoughts turned to the next game.

Our biggest win was at home to Droylsden, who always tried to play football, but they overplayed with the players they had and we swarmed all over them to win 6-3, with Lloydy scoring a hat-trick. It really could have been ten that day. We even played the last 15 minutes with Lee Mc in goal after we lost Chris Sanna to a back injury, and Macca took great delight afterwards in telling us how he kept a clean sheet.

The goalkeeper situation was to cost us in the next game as due to international clearance issues we were struggling to get in a replacement of the required quality.

Even though we were playing in an English league we needed international clearance to sign players because we were under the Welsh FA, and we had a game 48 hours after our keeper had got injured. I was on the phone non-stop trying to get a goalkeeper who was somewhere near our budget, but had drawn blank after blank.

Danny Meadowcroft, our non-league guru, told me there was a keeper at Hyde who would do us a job for a couple of games. 'He's six foot six; he's a big lad,' he said.

Danny's knowledge of players had been spot on in the past. The only problem was he must have previously seen this keeper on either a very, very good day or Danny had been out for a very good night the night before and was still recovering.

The warm-up didn't show any sign of the problems that were going to come in the game. I was expecting him to be a bit rusty after only playing reserve matches, but there's rusty and then there's Colwyn Bay away at Harrogate rusty. In the first minute Harrogate looped a ball into our penalty area and the keeper came flying out with one fist raised like Superman. If he had had a big S on his top though it would have stood for something else.

We were one down in the first minute. I stood on the touchline almost frozen to the spot and without even turning my head I said, 'Fuckin' hell, we're in trouble here with Stu.' He didn't say a word back. He didn't need to. He just looked straight ahead thinking the same as me.

We were right, and were 3-0 down at half-time with the back four in disarray nervous with about what was behind them. It went from bad to worse in the second half and we lost 4-0. The keeper gifted them another goal and I came on and missed a penalty. I never listened to Danny about a keeper ever again!

Just four days later we were due to play full-time Conference National side Lincoln City and a keeper was an absolute priority. Lee McEvilly was more likely to put the gloves on again than the lad who played at Harrogate.

I brought in Jack Cudworth from Macclesfield Town and he proved to be an excellent signing for a few months. Not only was he a good keeper, but his character was exactly what we needed. He was vocal, an organiser, full of energy and I liked him a lot.

We were struggling with a few injuries but it was the week in which I thought I had clinched the signing of a future England international defender.

We needed a centre-half and I had been to watch Oldham's reserves, where I liked the look of a young lad called James Tarkowski. A former team-mate of mine, Lee Duxbury, was in charge of the team and rang me later that evening to say the player fancied coming on loan for a month and that he would clear everything with the first-team manager the following day.

Unfortunately for us, Oldham lost a couple of players to injury in training that week and the deal fell through. Tarkowski was a sub for Oldham that weekend instead of playing for Colwyn Bay. Since then, he has become an established Premier League player worth millions of pounds and has appeared for England. It's amazing how little incidents and timing like that can shape a young player's future.

With us down to the bare bones at the back for the Lincoln game, Lee Mc was to play centre-half – well for about eight minutes anyway.

Lincoln had a couple of pacy strikers and here was no way Macca was going to chase them all game. It was one of those 'I'll let him know I'm there moments' as right next to the touchline he shoulder-barged the forward into the advertising boards.

In fact, I'm being too kind there: he shoulder-barged him through the advertising boards! It was a straight red card without any doubt and left us with ten men against a full-time team from the league above. We went on to lose 3-1. At least his sending-off would save me a few quid in the budget that week because of his fine for the red card.

As well as losing Lee for three games through suspension we also lost Danny Lloyd, as he impressed Lincoln enough for them to make an approach to sign him. He was a young player desperate to play full-time football so I was never going to stand in his way. I was delighted for him as he had worked very hard at his game and deserved to move up.

We managed to pull off the highest-profile signing in the club's history shortly after Christmas as I brought former Chelsea and Leicester City defender Frank Sinclair to Colwyn Bay.

Frank had been playing for Hendon, combining that with doing some media work for his old club Chelsea. My brother, who I should have employed as my southern scout (on no pay, of course!), had seen Sinclair playing for Hendon and said he looked in good shape and that he was still based in the north-west after previously appearing for Wrexham.

I got in touch with Frank and the deal was done quite quickly. It wasn't quite the money he was on at Chelsea that we thrashed out in his car at Kings School Chester, where we trained, but we were delighted to sign him. The chairman saw it as a big coup and some publicity for the club.

Frank fitted in perfectly to the dressing room – there were no airs and graces about him, despite the clubs he had played for – and he was great to work with.

Frank's first game was away at Altrincham, where he was seen as public enemy number one after an incident there the previous season with Wrexham. He went straight into another makeshift back four with captain Danny Meadowcroft unable to play and fellow centre-back Matty Hughes injured. We had lost three successive league games so I also went back to two up front and played myself alongside Rob Hopley.

Tactically it was difficult for us as a lot of teams had that bit more quality than us, so we had to be organised and compact while still having the freedom to get forward and score goals.

At Altrincham we were like Kevin Keegan's Newcastle teams – we'll just score more than we concede! Going forward we were excellent, but Altrincham were among the league's top scorers and we were too open, with only two central midfielders and our wide men not tucking in enough, and with half an hour to play we were 3-2 down.

As a player-manager your thoughts are different to the other players on the pitch. How can I change it? Should I take myself off? This could be our fourth defeat in a row.

You start moaning at referees and the opposition (I always did anyway!) while all these thoughts are going around your head trying to find a solution to getting back in the game.

Hopley brought us level at 3-3 and deep into injury time a corner caused a scramble in the Altrincham box and the script was written for debutant Sinclair to hook the ball home and, despite being booed for the full 90 minutes, he ran off with the biggest smile on his face, chased by myself, all the players and most of the dugout as we won 4-3. Who says football outside the Premier League doesn't matter?

That game was the start of a run that went a long way to securing our status as a Conference North club. In the next game we went away to Eastwood Town with another new signing. I brought in a winger called Shelton Payne, who had impressed me, and he was the quickest player I had ever seen. He made Usain Bolt look slow. As Eastwood tired, he was perfect to bring on and got to a ball he shouldn't have been quick enough to get to and was tripped in the box. Fraser McLachlan did the rest, nonchalantly passing the penalty home to give us two successive wins away from home.

We then drew 0-0 with Vauxhall, won 1-0 at Worcester City and then beat Boston United 3-2 at home.

Our final game of the month was away at Stalybridge Celtic and we were superb in winning 4-0, with Hopley scoring a nine-minute hat-trick. We were 'very lucky', though, according to the opposition bench when I and Stu shook hands with them at the final whistle. Lucky will do me every week if it results in four goals and a clean sheet.

Either way, that win and run of results had brought 16 points out of 18 and we had gone unbeaten in six games which earned me the manager of the month award from the league in just my third month in charge. I was very proud of that achievement.

The curse of that award was to strike a week later as we played one of the top sides, Nuneaton Borough. We had been successful that month with two up front, and I had played in all six games too, but I changed that against Nuneaton thinking we would need more players in the middle of the pitch. The approach backfired.

Rather than carrying on with what had brought us success, I started to overthink and thought more about the opposition instead of what we were good at. We were 4-0 down at half-time and the curse had well and truly hit. The second half would be nothing more than damage limitation.

I put myself on at half-time. It was my team that was four goals down, so it was only right I got out there and worked with them. We eventually lost 6-1 but tensions were high in the dressing room afterwards.

Lee Mc had been an unused sub and with about five minutes to go I glanced at the bench and saw Macca sneaking a look at his phone, which he had taken out in his pocket. He shouldn't have had his phone anyway, but in the situation it was disrespectful. He was either checking the day's football results or telling his Mrs to put his tea on, but it was wrong and he knew that.

As we got back to the dressing room, I should have given myself time to calm down and thought properly about why we had just been heavily beaten.

It certainly wasn't because Lee was on the phone but I went after him straight away, telling him he was out of order. He came back at me and it started to get heated then, as I walked towards him, he got up and walked towards me.

Anyone who knows the two of us knows it would have been heavyweight vs lightweight. Fortunately for me, Frank and Danny Meads jumped in between us and I lived to fight another day.

We decided the day after that we would part company, but I bumped into Lee a few months later when he was with Fylde and we had a laugh about it. Football has never been personal for me. The number of arguments and near fights that players have in moments like that is very large and if you held a grudge nobody would ever speak.

I see Lee often at football academies these days and we always have a chat. It shows how people's characters are affected and change in sport. It becomes a very emotional game and the best players and managers often find a way of taking the emotion out of the big moments.

We got back on track with a goalless draw away at Histon in the next game, and then came a 4-1 home win against Bishop's Stortford where I got my sixth goal of the season and an excellent future Premier League striker, Dwight Gayle, scored for the visitors.

That match also saw the league's lowest attendance of the season with just 141 supporters turning up. Granted, there was no away support as who is going to travel from Bishop's Stortford on a Tuesday night, and the weather was atrocious, but it was so telling that Colwyn Bay were never going to have the structure to compete in a division with former Football League clubs.

We then received news that rocked us. Under Conference regulations our Llanelian Road ground didn't have enough seats and to avoid being demoted down the leagues we had to build a new stand in two months at a cost of £70,000. We were about £30,000 short.

The chairman, directors and supporters were brilliant, and everybody pulled together to fundraise and do the initial labour and spadework themselves. It was a very hectic time and occasionally the building of the stand would eat into the playing budget, but it was necessary as we had all worked too hard to be demoted for non-playing reasons – and at least it meant that the seats we got in the Damien Allen transfer could be put to good use.

On a matchday, the way the budget worked was that only the 16 players in the squad got paid. We only carried an 18-man squad anyway as it was difficult asking lads to travel to training twice a week if they weren't getting paid and when they could be playing for another club. Our location also made it difficult for us as travelling had an impact on what we could offer players financially.

We had our most difficult run of the season at the same time as we were having to find money for the new stand, starting with a 1-0 defeat at Solihull Moors. We were starting to get dragged into a relegation battle with the league; it was close from mid-table to the final relegation place. When we had beaten Stalybridge 4-0 at the end of January we had moved into sixth place, just one place outside the play-offs, but it was so tight that a couple of defeats found us back in the bottom half of the table.

Our next game saw us beaten 5-0 at home to Hinckley United and I didn't help matters as I was shown the first red card of my career for retaliating to a couple of poor tackles by grabbing a defender by the throat.

It was the only time I was sent off. We had just gone a goal down and I was too emotionally charged in games, unable to separate playing and managing. To make matters worse, as I was involved in my scuffle, there was another coming together in what was a bad-tempered game as Gaz Evans became involved in an incident with his opposite number.

It is a horrible feeling being shown a red card, knowing you have let your team-mates down, but doing it as a manager is even worse. As I started my walk off the pitch I heard a cheer, turned to see another red card being shown and thought, 'Well at least it's ten v ten.' It wasn't.

The second red had been shown to Evo. In 60 seconds we were down to nine men with 65 minutes left to play. We went on to lose heavily with another Premier League-bound player, Andre Gray, taking full advantage of the spaces on the pitch, while I and Evo were now banned for three games when we were needed the most.

Football management is a funny job. One minute you're high and the next you're low and when you are winning games everyone is stood with you, but when you are losing it's the loneliest job in the world. And in the middle of this run it felt pretty lonely.

There are no days off as you have to be involved in everything, and after another defeat at Gainsborough, this time 1-0, the club had organised a sponsored walk up Mount Snowdon to raise funds for the building of the stand. About 30 of us – me, my brother, directors and supporters – took to the mountain the day after the defeat, which at least cleared my head for a couple of hours on a beautiful day.

I was suspended at Workington and, even though I was manager, I wasn't allowed on the bench due to my ban. There was no money in the budget at Colwyn Bay for earpieces for me and Stu to communicate either like you see on the television!

Despite Karl Noon scoring an excellent goal we lost 3-1 and we were now just outside the relegation zone. We were sinking and at that moment both I and the team couldn't arrest that slide.

We simply could not go down. I wasn't someone who quit. I had battled through enough hard times in my career, but I did say to the chairman if he wanted me to step down after the six consecutive defeats I would understand. He dismissed it immediately and I was grateful to him for that.

We had three games left and at that stage four points would guarantee us safety, but with teams at the bottom playing each other, every point would count.

I spoke to some of my previous managers and coaches who had been in similar situations on how they went about things, and I also talked at length with Hughie McAuley about how to play a back three as I thought it would benefit us.

Frank Sinclair rang me to suggest the same and also thought I should be playing myself, so I got my boots on again after my ban.

We also had more goalkeeping problems with injury, but we had young Andy Metcalfe ready to step in. Andy was very inexperienced and had only really played at reserve level, but he had improved a lot in that season. The transfer deadline had been and gone so Andy was thrown in at the deep end and he was superb in those last three games under a lot of pressure, growing in confidence with each appearance.

The first game was at home to Harrogate, who like us were in a battle against the drop. We were excellent in the game and deserved more than the point we got in a 2-2 draw.

Mike Lea gave us a half-time lead but we conceded a sloppy equaliser. We thought we had won it when Frank scored in the 87th minute only for Harrogate to level a minute later. It was doubly frustrating as every result had gone for us that day and had we held on to the three points we would have been mathematically safe with two games left to play.

We went to high-flying Nuneaton in the next game knowing that a win guaranteed us safety but despite leading for most of the game through Rob Hopley, we conceded a freak late own goal and had to settle for a point again.

As management, Stu and I were almost playing mind games with the players after those two games in the dressing room. 'That will be the point that keeps us up.' 'Its massive. Other teams are seeing us outplay top teams and pick up points.' At the same time at the back of your mind as you are talking, you're trying to convince yourself, 'We'll be all right, won't we?'

Gloucester City at home was the final game of the season. The new stand was built and open for the game as the chairman had worked wonders getting it completed, so we were safe on that score. We just had to do the business on the pitch.

Seven teams could still have filled the final relegation place, with two teams already down. Imagine how many times the 'as it stands' table would have changed on Sky Sports that day?

Gloucester were safe in mid-table, but that could work both ways. Maybe they wouldn't play at the same intensity that they would if they needed to win, or maybe they would play with freedom under no pressure and want to finish the season with a victory. But it was about what we did, not them.

The team talk was all about starting well. It was so important. The first ten minutes could go a long way to deciding the result.

'Start well, score the first goal, believe the goals will come,' was the message over and over.

We couldn't have started any better as we scored within the opening 90 seconds. A long ball into the channel, which I flicked inside, was smashed into the top corner by Hops. The feeling was almost as good as the final whistle against FC United the previous season. Almost.

Fifteen minutes later it was two as I was shoved over in the box and Fraser calmly rolled the penalty home. Less than a minute later it was 3-0 as Evo curled a sublime left-foot shot around the keeper from outside the box and on the stroke of half-time John McKenna made it four. We were nearly home and dry.

'I don't know what all the fuckin' panic is about,' Fraser McLachlan said in his typical laid-back style as he sat down with a shrug of his shoulders. 'We were never going to go down, you know.'

We saw the game out, winning 4-2 after conceding twice in the final ten minutes, but we were safe and would be playing Conference North football again in the following season.

Back in the dressing room I thanked the players. They had worked hard and given their all, even when results hadn't always gone our way. It was a satisfying way to end the season. Relief was the right word. Maybe I would allow myself to switch off for a week. I doubted it, but maybe.

With the win against Gloucester we finished in 12th place on 53 points, a reassuring eight places and five points above the relegation zone. Maybe Fraser had been right, what was all the fuss about?

The season finished with me having a kickabout on the pitch with Josh and Olivia. My first season as a manager was over. It had been stressful, emotional and tiring with just a little bit of enjoyment thrown in. Oh, and a lot of relief! Let's do it all again next season.

18

It's time for a change

THE FOLLOWING season was always going to be as tough as, if not tougher than, the one we had just survived.

More big clubs like Chester FC had come into the league and with them being local to us, that made it even more difficult for us to attract the best players in our region. Oxford City were another new club, and they were full time.

Our playing budget had gone up by £100 to £3,000 a week. Every little helped I suppose.

Barry Taylor, who had been on the staff the previous season as physio, was to combine his medical duties with helping me a bit more, especially watching our opposition before we played them, and Baz was a big help that year. The chairman also brought in Welshman Gus Williams, although that was an appointment I wasn't sure about.

Gus is a lovely fella and we worked well together. I liked him, but the chairman was starting to pick who he wanted at the club rather than me choosing my own staff. Bob Paton made it clear to me that summer that he didn't want my assistant or my physio at the club. He said he personally didn't value what they brought.

I disagreed but said if he was adamant then I wanted £200 a week more so I could bring in an assistant with 20 years of experience in that role and who would help both me and Colwyn

Bay. The answer was always no, so there was no way I was going to let staff that I trusted leave without having an experienced replacement that I had chosen.

We lost a couple of players that summer, but I brought in four I really wanted: Tom Smyth, a centre-half from Northwich; Sean Williams, a playmaker in midfield from Skelmersdale United; Danny Lloyd returned from Lincoln City; and at the last minute my number-one target Kevin Holsgrove joined from Vauxhall Motors.

We had brought in four players who would improve us and the signing of centre-forward Holsgrove was one that I was delighted with.

I wanted to put him on a contract rather than him being a non-contract player, but that was stopped by those above me. If a player is on non-contract forms it means that any club can put in seven days' notice in for him and he is then free to leave at the end of that time period if he wishes to.

A contract ties that player to your club and prevents the seven-day rule from being effective. The only issue with a contracted player is that if he is injured and doesn't play, he still had to be paid. The chairman felt that players coming in had to earn contracts with how they did at our club, but for me Holsgrove wasn't a risk. I'd seen enough of him over the years to know that he would make a massive difference with good players around him.

We had a good squad but Holsgrove would be so important to us and I felt it was short-sighted by the club not to have him secured to us.

Pre-season went well. We went to Welsh Premier League team Airbus, managed by my former boss Andy Preece, and were excellent in winning 6-1, and then led 3-0 against a young Manchester City side before we changed most of our team at half-time, ready for the start of the season three days later, and ended up losing 4-3. But we looked ready for what lay ahead.

Our first game was at home to Solihull Moors, and I couldn't have asked for any more from the players. We were 2-0 up at half-time with Sean Williams scoring a goal-of-the-season contender and Danny Lloyd netting on his return to the club. Holsgrove added a third as we won 3-1 and he and Rob Hopley looked a formidable partnership up front.

I was struggling with a toe injury that was requiring injections and I wouldn't be in the squad for the opening six games, but I was more than happy to miss out if Kev and Hops played like that every week.

Our next match was away at Halifax, whose squad could easily have competed in the division above and were full of former Football League players. We went with a plan to defend deep and hit them on the break with Lloydy and Kev's pace. The lads were brilliant again and Holsgrove scored a late winner as little Colwyn Bay went top of the league.

Our excellent start continued as we went away to big-spending Chester. Off the pitch it was David v Goliath in every way, even though we were in the same division, but we were as good as Chester that day. There was a great atmosphere with over 2,000 fans in the ground and despite falling behind from a set-piece, we levelled when Holsgrove scored a fine solo goal.

We ended up losing 2-1, conceding another set-piece goal and missed two golden chances to level late on, but the first three matches of the season had given us real belief.

An incident in the 90th minute, though, became a major talking point and would impact us for games to come.

A long ball by a Chester player bounced just in our half as we pushed forward and their winger, who was stood at least ten yards offside, put his hands up to say he wasn't involved in the play.

Due to the new rule, because he didn't touch the ball, the linesman didn't flag for offside, so the player then turned and chased the ball. Our goalkeeper Chris Sanna raced out of his box and a few seconds later the linesman decided now was the right time to raise his flag. It was far too late as two committed players collided and there was a sickening head clash.

Chris was knocked out and badly concussed and we were then without him for a month. It was unnecessary and endangered both players because the linesman couldn't sense the danger of not putting his flag up even though everybody could see the player was ten yards offside.

I went to see the referee after the match and an FA assessor just happened to be there and agreed that the rule was dangerous, but the linesman said his hands were tied. Chris had been put in a dangerous situation and it had a massive impact on us.

It was a Bank Holiday weekend when we played Chester, so we had another fixture two days later against Stalybridge Celtic. We couldn't sign a goalkeeper on loan as the Welsh FA offices were closed and we needed international clearance to bring anybody in, so Andy Metcalfe, who had performed well at the end of the previous season, was thrown in again.

The problem was that he hadn't played much in pre-season and he wasn't match sharp.

Again we were excellent and went 2-0 up through Frank Sinclair and Gaz Evans, but the game changed on one silly decision by Kevin Holsgrove. On the stroke of half-time he chased a ball into the corner and inexplicably took a wild swipe at the defender running alongside him, off the ball, so was rightly shown a red card.

Off the pitch Kev was the nicest fella in the world so it was totally out of character and he was full of remorse at half-time knowing he had let the team down.

We were coasting at 2-0, but a Stalybridge goal 20 minutes from time changed the game and we looked nervous.

I was too late at reacting to put another man in the middle of midfield, and before I made the tactical change Stalybridge were level going into the last few minutes after a mistake by Andy. Worse was to follow as in injury time the young keeper tried to punch a corner away and the ball came off his fist into the net for an own goal as we lost 3-2 from a comfortable winning position.

Andy was struggling with his confidence that week so we brought in Dom Comrie, who had been at Preston and came with good recommendations. But his debut away at Worcester City lasted all of ten minutes when he brought down their centre-forward to concede a penalty and was shown a red card.

Another dismissal and 80 minutes of centre-back Tom Smyth playing in goal saw us lose 2-0.

We had to stop losing men, which was my responsibility, but this goalkeeping chain of events would have been avoidable if the linesman had raised his flag at Chester. These were the tiny bits of luck that a small club like us needed to go in our favour rather than against us.

After the game at Worcester, we lost 2-0 at home to both Boston and Guiseley, and what I feared with Holsgrove transpired when he impressed the Guiseley manager Steve Kittrick and they put seven days' notice in on him. My heart sank when I received the phone call and I was fuming because it had been so preventable. We had lost a top player.

I tried to persuade him to stay as I knew that at Guiseley he would just be another squad player. With us he was so important, and I wanted to build the team around his partnership with Rob Hopley, and play Sean Williams behind them. Guiseley, however, doubled his money and I had no answer to that. That was always going to be the danger if we weren't prepared to forward-plan and secure our best players. It was a major blow and something that was so avoidable.

We stopped the run of poor results against one of the fancied teams that season, Brackley Town, drawing 1-1 at home before losing to Guiseley in the FA Cup and missing out on valuable prize money.

The next two games were absolutely vital for us as we were playing bottom side Hinckley twice in a week, because we were both out of the FA Cup. We were in the final relegation spot with just seven points and we simply had to win both matches.

I was starting to get vibes off the chairman, following a meeting about the number of red cards we had been shown, that if things didn't improve then my time would be up.

I agreed that results determine managers' futures, but we were Colwyn Bay and were playing at the highest level in the club's history and staying in that division should be considered successful. Bob Paton, however, claimed that if we lost matches then we lost supporters. We had a hardcore support of around 250 who were brilliant, but we could have won 5-0 every week playing like Brazil and we wouldn't have gained any more – that was obvious from the play-off-winning season.

Football-wise, Colwyn Bay had reached a ceiling and it was just a question of how many years the club could stay at this level. It was a challenge that me as a manager, the players and the directors always met head on, but the board had to be more realistic as to what we were able to achieve with the resources and structure we had.

With Holsgrove gone I started myself at home to Hinckley but we looked nervous and found ourselves two goals down. I made one of my better decisions at half-time, bringing on a third striker in Matty Berkeley, who had signed in the summer but hadn't shown enough in the opening weeks. He was a talented player who needed a rocket up him at times, but he came on and changed the game. He scored within five minutes and was excellent as two further goals in as many minutes from Rob Hopley and Gaz Evans turned things around and gave us a massive three points.

A week later came the return fixture and Matty had done enough to keep his place. We started well, going 2-0 up within 25 minutes. After Hinckley got one back we weathered a storm. Substitute Jon Breeze added a late third and two wins in a week gave the league table a much better look about it.

There were still rumblings from above, however, with the chairman continuing to tell me I had surrounded myself with the wrong backroom staff. I spent one weekend at loggerheads with him over his threat to sack one of my assistants for taking the wrong pint at the bar after the game, levelling an accusation of theft against him.

If you don't want him at the club that's up to you, it's your club, but don't try and get rid of someone for mistakenly taking the wrong drink. You couldn't make it up at one stage. If we won then the response wasn't positive about the game, it was negative about something else.

After our two victories we showed our inconsistencies and with Frank Sinclair suspended we lost 2-0 at Droylsden and 2-1 at home to Bradford Park Avenue.

The Bradford game saw striker Jamie Rainford make his first appearance after signing on loan from Halifax Town. Jamie was a goalscorer and had been a man in demand in non-league a few seasons earlier but had then changed clubs a fair bit.

Other managers I spoke to advised me against signing him. I was told he was always moaning, didn't work hard enough and didn't have the right attitude. I knew we would get goals from him, though, and with him knowing a few of the boys in the squad I felt he would settle in quickly.

He came in and, despite what people had told me, he wasn't a minute's bother and worked hard in training and games. Did he moan? Yes, but show me a striker who is happy when he isn't scoring goals. He was the type who needed an arm round him, cajoling the best out of him, not giving him a bollocking. If he was scoring goals he was happy, but his attitude was never in question and he did what I signed him to do, score goals.

Our next match was at full-time Oxford City. It was a difficult place to go, but we enjoyed playing away from home. It suited our style as a team. We scored a brilliant goal when Gaz Evans hit the top corner following a flowing team move, and Jamie also scored his first goal for the club. Fellow loanee Cameron Darkwah did well to win a penalty, and Jamie, who had just come on as a 67th-minute substitute, grabbed the ball and smashed it to the keeper's right to score with his first touch of the game.

It turned out to be the winner as we gained another valuable three points. There was still no positivity from the chairman and the directors. At the end of the game, it was, 'We nearly threw that away, didn't we?' We had just won three out of the last five games, two of them away from home, but to that the answer was, 'It was only Hinckley.'

The next two fixtures didn't help as we lost 3-1 at Gainsborough Trinity and 2-1 at home to Harrogate prior to Christmas, and going into our home game with fellow strugglers Histon I said to the staff I thought it was 'win or bust' for us.

Despite conceding early on we were a real threat and led at half-time with Rainford and Hopley both scoring. Rainford added his second of the game and it was a well-deserved victory.

We were then due to play Vauxhall twice over the holiday period but all of a sudden, I wasn't allowed to renew Jamie Rainford's loan spell, which had finished after the Histon game.

He was desperate to stay and to keep playing, I was desperate to keep him, and Halifax manager Neil Aspin was more than happy for him to stay another month, but now there was 'no money' to extend the loan spell of a player who had scored three times in his last four appearances and it seemed that my relationship with the chairman, and one of the directors in particular, had deteriorated.

The Boxing Day fixture at Vauxhall finished 1-1, but that told half the story. With Rainford's loan spell not extended and a raft of injuries I started myself and on the bench as was my 44-year-old assistant manager Stuart Barlow, just so we had our full quota of subs, and we scored early through Liverpool lad Luke Holden.

Luke could play. He was the oldest-looking 24-year-old I'd ever seen, but he had a left foot like a wand. He also moaned more than me on the pitch, which was some feat!

We played well but I missed a golden opportunity to make the points safe late on. I was running on empty by then, having hardly played that season, but I still should have taken the chance. Unfortunately, for the next ten minutes one of our directors decided to let me and our bench know that I should have scored.

I can take that from a supporter, but a director should be showing more professionalism than shouting 'get Newby off' from the stand. To add insult to injury, we conceded a 96th-minute equaliser when a midfielder tried to overplay, and we had dropped two points.

I confronted the director after the game and in no uncertain terms told him how unprofessional he had been. I probably would have been best keeping my cool, but after the late equaliser my emotions got the better of me and I was at a stage where I knew what was coming if we didn't beat Vauxhall at home on New Year's Day.

My last game as manager of Colwyn Bay was on 1 January 2013. Again, I started, and Stuart Barlow made up the bench, and after a really poor first half we found ourselves 2-0 down at half-time.

We spoke candidly in the dressing room knowing that it hadn't been good enough, but if we scored the first goal in the second half we would get something out of the game. As me, Stu and Barry went into the staff dressing room, I noticed that my phone kept flashing.

Nobody ever rang me on a matchday afternoon. Nobody had rung me at that time since mobile phones were invented. Everyone knew where I would be at that time on a matchday.

I never looked at my phone at half-time, but that day I did. There was a short text message from a player who had once been a team-mate saying 'be careful' as his manager had asked if he was interested in going on loan to Colwyn Bay because Colwyn's new manager had been ringing managers in the Welsh Premier League to see which clubs had players available.

He even gave me the new manager's name. I had to read it about three times. I felt numb. I was about to go out and play in the second half having effectively just been sacked.

I was on autopilot and just played football. A lot better than I had done in the first half as it turned out. I crossed for Rob Hopley to head us back into the game and then five minutes later Danny Lloyd brought us level from the penalty spot. We were level just ten minutes into the second half. What if we came back from 2-0 down to win the game? Will they still sack me? Those were the thoughts going around in my head as I played the second half.

The chairman and directors must have been breathing a sigh of relief when just minutes later an individual error at the back gave Vauxhall the lead again and they quickly added a fourth as we lost 4-2.

I spoke to the players calmly after the match, not mentioning what I knew, but they all knew how big the two Vauxhall encounters were for us as a staff and the mood was sombre.

Everyone had gone and I was still sat in my kit on the physio bed lost in my own thoughts an hour after the final whistle. I was only interrupted by Airbus manager Andy Preece ringing to tell me the same as what I'd read at half-time as the 'new' manager had also rung him that morning, and again by the director I had fallen out with at Vauxhall to tell me that the chairman wanted to see me.

I had no problem with any of the directors who thought a change in manager was needed; it was their club and they had to decide what was right, but some of the people at the top acted with no dignity. The club had every right to set things in motion regarding finding a new manager, even appointing one privately, but be professional. Make sure it isn't made public until the current manager has been told he is losing his job.

I spoke to Stuart and Baz later that night, but they had no contact from the club, not even a phone call, until they received a letter six days later saying their services were no longer required.

They both deserved better than that for the hard work they had put in during the last 14 months.

The chairman asked me to resign, but I refused for two reasons. Firstly, I knew what I knew and because of that I wasn't going to make it easy for him, and secondly, because I hadn't lost the players. They were still playing for me, still working hard and giving me everything. We were down to the bare bones, with loan players sent back to their parent clubs, and a 44-year-old on the bench.

If I had lost the dressing room I would have resigned. I hadn't. The chairman told me that in that case he had no alternative but to sack me.

'It's time for a change,' he said. The words went right through me. I was just staring into space. I told him he was wrong as I shook his hand and just walked out. I was on autopilot. I was in the room, but my head wasn't.

What was the point in arguing? I wasn't going to stand there and beg. I wasn't in a good place. I could have gone absolutely crazy in that room the way things had been done, but it would have been the worst idea in the world as I honestly think that had I let my true feelings out the situation wouldn't have ended well.

I can tell you that being sacked is one of the worst feelings in the world, no matter the level of the club that you are managing. It is a horrendous feeling.

That defeat had left us on 20 points from 19 games. We were in 17th position, five points outside the relegation zone. We were probably above where we should have been at that level. We were putting fires out week after week.

I made mistakes, plenty of them, and being older and wiser now I would do many things differently, but the people at the top were expecting things that a club the size of Colwyn Bay simply couldn't do at the level we were competing at.

I had taken charge of the club for 53 games. The man who replaced me lasted 49 less than me and was sacked after just four matches in charge, with the team losing all four and scoring just once.

Just three seasons later the club had been relegated twice. It's not easy, this football management.

Colwyn Bay was a club that started so well for me. I have some amazing memories from there, both as a player and manager. The goals, the victories and the people as well. But the overriding memory for me personally, because of how it all ended, will always be, rightly or wrongly, that I failed.

19

Keep playing for as long as you can

AFTER LOSING my job at Colwyn Bay I felt I had no other option but to carry on playing. There was no way I could let my football career finish on that note, and I knew I wasn't in a great place mentally, so playing football would at least give me some kind of focus.

A mate of mine, Lee Smith, was on the staff at Evo-Stik Division One North club Warrington Town and he gave me a call asking if I would be interested in joining. After a chat with manager Shaun Reid I signed straight away.

To be honest I was looking forward to just playing again and letting someone else have the pressure of picking teams and worrying about results. I was nearly 35 by now, not as quick, not as fit, and if truth be told not as enthusiastic after the last few months at Colwyn Bay.

Warrington was my home town. I was born there and lived there until I was nine. While we lived there, if we weren't at Anfield watching Liverpool then our Saturday afternoons were often spent watching Warrington at Cantilever Park and I had played at the ground for the town's district team back in the 1980s as a kid, so I'd already scored my first goal there.

I knew a few of the players, too, as I had signed both David Mannix and Fraser McLachlan while I was manager at Colwyn.

I also knew of the majority of the other lads. Most of them were Scousers and anyone with connections to the city will tell you that being good at football is almost a form of currency in Liverpool. If you're half-decent most people will know of you.

There were some really good players at Warrington; some were technically excellent and individually outstanding, but as a team we didn't quite gel.

Most of the lads had been in non-league football for a long time and it was a good life for them. Working full time during the week and then picking up a few hundred quid, to essentially play football with your mates at the weekend, isn't bad, really.

We had leaders in Craig Robinson and Jay McCarten at the back, Peter Doogan in midfield could play and put a foot in, captain David Mannix had been in the 2005 Liverpool Champions League Final matchday squad, Scott Metcalfe and Liam Dawson were technically excellent and Ciaran Kilheeney up front was someone who regularly scored 25 goals a season at that level.

Warrington were a club on the up and were just starting to have a real go at progressing through the leagues but they just needed a few more fans through the gates, although as a rugby town that was always difficult.

Shaun Reid made sure the football side of things was done right. He had been a professional at a few Football League clubs in the north-west and coming from a real footballing family he was a hard taskmaster. If Reidy didn't like something you did on a Saturday afternoon, he'd make sure he told you and every supporter in the ground with how loud he berated you, and if he really didn't like what you had done, he'd kick you up in the air for it on a Monday night at training.

He was as passionate a manager as I ever worked with and sometimes he probably went overboard in the dressing room, as we all do at times – especially as managers – but he had standards on the pitch and in training and he wanted them met.

He knew his football inside out and had fantastic knowledge about the game, but he got frustrated when people didn't care as much as he did.

Away from the pitch he would sit and talk all day about football, and he was Warrington's manager when they beat Exeter City in the FA Cup live on the television not so long ago.

During that 2013/14 season we had such a turnover of players that it was difficult to find the right blend among the lads. There were often up to three or four new players at training each week and that made it harder for a settled team to gel together.

I scored five goals for the Yellows – against New Mills, Salford City, Burscough, Wakefield and Ossett Town. The Ossett goal was particularly significant for me, because it was the last one I would score in proper competitive football, and because it was the first goal time I had ever scored in the FA Cup.

It was also one of the best goals I scored in my career. I was on as a second-half sub with Warrington trailing 1-0. Ossett's keeper punched a deep cross to the edge of the box and I anticipated where it would land, adjusting my feet and catching it perfectly on the volley for it to hit the inside of the post and fly into the top corner.

We were desperate for a cup run and all the lads to a man jumped all over me in celebration. It was a great feeling as I came to the end of my career and one that I'll always remember.

Unfortunately we lost the replay 3-1, but having been drawn away to Colwyn Bay in the next round it might not have been a bad thing that we were knocked out as it would have been an interesting reunion for me.

So my last goal in competitive football was on 28 September 2013. I left Warrington in November that year after a few more appearances but I wasn't ready to finish playing totally just yet.

20

Royton away, two o'clock kick-off

IT WAS time to go back to why we had all started playing when we were kids, simply because we loved the game.

A good mate of mine, Richard Birtwistle, whose son played in the same junior team as my son, had been trying to convince me for months to play for the team he managed, Walshaw Sports A in the Manchester Amateur League.

The A team was only the third team of the club, but we became known as the 'Legends'. In our own dressing room anyway! It was back to the days of having to pay to play, but for just over two and a half years I enjoyed it as much as anything in my career.

Our home ground up in the hills of Bacup was a far cry from Anfield or even Gigg Lane, and the weather up there could give you all four seasons of the year in 90 minutes, but it was the next place to go and try and score goals.

Birty and fellow manager Philip 'Feej' Williams had the right balance between wanting to win, being as professional as possible and realising it was as much about camaraderie as anything else.

There was me and Lee Connell who had both been professionals, with Lee – 'The Colonel' – also being a former team-mate at Bury. A couple of the lads had played local non-league football in the North West Counties League, but aside from that the players were mostly in their 30s and 40s just wanting a game of football.

I paid my first batch of subs on 15 February 2014 and pulled on the black and white stripes of Walshaw against Springhead. I got kicked all over the pitch for 90 minutes, argued with the opposition, got called every name under the sun, moaned at the ref and scored a goal as we won 5-2 – and I absolutely loved it!

I ran myself into the ground even at that level and it felt great getting home on a Saturday evening aching all over but feeling like I had done something worthwhile.

I'll always maintain that football is a drug to me, an addiction, a way of life. Through the bad spells in my career I couldn't live with it, but I found it even harder to live without it when I wasn't playing.

The feeling and the challenge of competing against defenders, the desire to work hard, to win and, most importantly, that feeling of scoring a goal were things I still needed in my life for my own mental wellbeing.

I'd never found football easy to deal with emotionally. Bad games in my playing days often led to a couple of days of me hardly talking. My head would hit the pillow at night and the whole game would be replayed in my mind; every pass, every chance. I know from speaking to other players and reading interviews that many footballers are the same, but I never found a way to deal with it. Mentally, football can get on top of you.

Without doubt, for well over a year after I left Colwyn Bay, I suffered with depression. I was never diagnosed with any illness because I never sought any medical advice or help, but at the time I knew, and looking back now it is even more obvious.

There were days when I would stay in the house all day, most of the time upstairs in the bedroom, and just shut myself away from everyone. My wife and the kids would go out on a Sunday and I would just find any excuse not to go with them. Deep down I wanted to, but I almost couldn't face going out.

I wasn't working full time then and just felt I had failed in my life. I hadn't had the career I wanted to have and that still played on my mind at times.

I wanted to put that right, and almost make up for it in management, but losing my job in the manner I had at Colwyn Bay had sent me spiralling downwards. It wasn't something I could just snap out of.

With everyone else I would try and be as positive as possible and attempt to smile through it, but for my own family it must have been very difficult because I just felt I had let them down. I was one of those people who when I used to hear someone say they were depressed I would just think, 'Oh get on with it!'

Only when you have struggled yourself do you realise that you can't just get on with it. Depression doesn't allow you to, and although there is now much better help for players suffering with mental health issues, there is still so much more that can be done. I know even my wife at times was thinking, 'You have us, do we not make you happy?'

I think what people close to those struggling fail to realise is that you think that everybody thinks of you in the same way that you see yourself. I saw myself as a failure, so that was exactly what I thought even Wendy and the children thought of me, and most days I couldn't always find a way of letting them in to my world.

I couldn't find a way out of it, and I didn't look for any professional help. However I genuinely think that playing for Walshaw helped me find my own way out of what I was struggling with. The lads at Walshaw would never have known what was going on in my mind, but they helped me more than they could ever realise.

Playing football and feeling better about myself helped me so much and slowly let me get to where I needed to be mentally.

Playing for Walshaw was different because all of a sudden, even at 36, I was above the level. The standard of the opposition at times wasn't great and I'd be scoring four or five in 10-2 victories against the likes of Chapeltown and Heywood, but there were some really close games against the better teams such as AVRO and Royton Town.

Royton became our bitter rivals, and the games were brutal every time. They played in the shadow of Oldham Athletic's ground and the fans would be walking past us on the way to the match watching two teams kick lumps out of each other.

Every game against Royton ended in a mass brawl and normally a few red cards. The problem in some of these leagues was that, although there are some good players who can play, there are also a lot of lads who think they can fight.

You would only have to tackle someone or even go past a player and they saw nothing wrong with wanting to two-foot you or taking you out with a clothesline – and then all hell would break loose.

I learnt very quickly to hurdle shortly after I signed for Walshaw. It was either that or end up with a broken leg. I would be in bits the following day hobbling about, but I couldn't wait for the next game and more of the same.

We arrived at one game and a few of their players said, 'Is that new young lad playing, the one who is rapid who scores every week that everyone is talking about?'

We could truthfully answer 'no' as I definitely wasn't young, and I didn't even think I was that quick anymore!

But all of a sudden I had become a marked man for the first time since I had played for Bury, and it was almost nice being spoken about again in that way. I would look forward to games as if they were the best part of the week again.

Scoring all five as we came back from 2-0 down against Royton to win 5-4, turning and scoring from the halfway line against Atherton, still getting pissed off with myself if I hadn't scored with ten minutes to go and then feeling relief when I finally got on the scoresheet; all great memories.

Why was it still so important to me? I realised at that stage that mentally, football was what held me together. That was the glue. If the football was going well everything else in my life fell into place and the world was a good place. If it wasn't going well, I could be a nightmare to be around, even though my career had finished and I was essentially 'playing for fun'.

The team spirit we had was absolutely brilliant. There were no egos, just a group of lads who wanted to win and stick together and those two and a half seasons were so enjoyable.

In that time we won a cup final, although strictly speaking I had registered too late for the cup that season and was playing as a ringer under a different name, so the authorities may still be looking into that one. There was panic written all over Birty's and Feej's faces when the league's committee members turned up to watch the final!

We also won the league twice, both of these legally, and yes it meant something to me even at that level.

By the time we won the league in 2016 most of the lads had decided that it was to be their last season. We were only the third team and the hierarchy at the club wanted a couple of the players to move up and play in the teams above, but it wasn't about that for us.

We were playing together as mates, and that was what was probably the most enjoyable thing about it. We would have run through brick walls for each other, and sometimes it felt like we were against AVRO and Royton Town.

So, the 'Legends' were no more and on 12 May 2016 I played my last game of football as we came back from 2-0 down to draw 2-2 at Breightmet on a Thursday night.

I scored 112 goals in 56 games for Walshaw. Finally, I had a goals-to-games ratio that would get me a big move! There was just nothing like scoring goals.

It still meant so much to me. I have coached, I have managed, but nothing will ever be able to fill the void of playing for me.

I often read and hear footballers say that the thing they miss the most is the dressing room and the team spirit and, yes, I have played in some teams where the dressing room was really enjoyable – Bury, Morecambe, Colwyn Bay and Walshaw Sports especially – but more than anything else I just miss playing football.

21

Arrhythmogenic right ventricular cardiomyopathy

ARVC. I had never heard of it. These days there is not one single day that the four letters don't cross my mind.

ARVC, going by its full name, is arrhythmogenic right ventricular cardiomyopathy. It is a condition in which, due to the walls of one of the chambers in your heart starting to stretch and scar, muscle turns to fat and the blood is not pumped round the heart as it should be, so the normal electrical rhythm of the heart is interrupted, causing major cardiac arrhythmias.

I was diagnosed with it on 21 March 2019 while still on the operating table at St George's Hospital in London.

It means that you are at increased risk of a sudden cardiac arrest, with death a likely outcome, and up to 80 per cent of people who have the condition never know they have as it is only discovered when a post-mortem is carried out. There is no cure for this progressive condition, which will only get worse as I get older. It is also genetic and both I and my wife pray it never affects our children the way it has me.

Some people are born with the ARVC gene but don't show symptoms until much later in life. In other people, particularly endurance athletes, the condition is occasionally shown to be 'exercise-induced ARVC'. We train our hearts so hard for such long periods that essentially we damage the muscle, and it looks like that could be what has happened to me.

I think about how many games of football I have played in my lifetime. As a young lad it would have been at least two at the weekend, sometimes three if another team asked me to play on a Sunday afternoon as well. As a youth player, there would be another two a week. Once I became a professional I played close to 300 first-team games in my career and another 130-plus in various reserve sides. Dropping into non-league saw me play another 170 times and then a further 55 for Walshaw in my final years as a player. So, from the age of 18 onwards, we are talking probably 700 appearances.

Add to that pre-season friendlies and then training sessions every day for 20 years or so, and that is a lot of work for anyone's heart to get through. As a footballer you don't think anything of it. You're programmed to do it; it becomes second nature.

Plenty of players played far more games than I did but the way I played, forever running channels and playing on the shoulder of the last defender, was constant high-intensity sprinting.

The surgeon gave me an explanation as to how ARVC comes out in some people and not others, even though they may carry the gene. If one person trained at high intensity and the other was someone who did very little exercise then the gene would likely lay dormant in the person who didn't exercise, but the high-intensity athlete would show symptoms.

The game I love, that became a drug to me, is more than likely the reason I have this heart condition that has changed my life.

It is the exact condition that in 2007 caused Seville player Antonio Puerta to collapse in a Spanish La Liga game while on the pitch. He later died in hospital aged just 22. It is also the same condition that caused England cricketer James Taylor to early retire early into his Test career after a major medical incident.

There are a few different types of cardiomyopathy, ARVC being one of the major ones. A different type of cardiomyopathy is what caused Fabrice Muamba to collapse on the pitch at White Hart Lane in 2012, in an incident the whole world remembers. That is how serious it is.

On the day of my diagnosis a defibrillator had just shocked me to prevent me from going into cardiac arrest, and as I lay on the operating table having just been told of the condition, the surgeon gave me even more life-changing news, 'You are going to need an ICD. An internal cardiac defibrillator implanted in your chest. One day it will save your life.'

It was a hell of a lot to take in while lying on the bed still feeling the after-effects of being shocked by a defibrillator.

'Just no more shocks,' I remember saying to him, half-smiling and just simply relieved that the operation was over.

And that was that. I was taken back to my hospital ward knowing that soon my chest would be cut open and a small metal machine would be placed next to my heart ready to save my life when it needed to. My life was about to change forever.

Later that afternoon the surgeon who had performed the operation came back to see Wendy and me and have a proper conversation about what was to happen next. Emotions were running quite high. I wasn't upset, just in shock. Dazed almost. You never think it will be you. I couldn't really digest everything that he was saying to me; my thoughts were more about what was going to come when the ICD was fitted. I remember Wendy asking most of the questions.

'Can he not have the ICD fitted when he has fully recovered from this surgery. Maybe in a few weeks?' she asked.

The answer was emphatic. 'I can't let him leave this hospital without having the defibrillator fitted,' he replied. 'He isn't walking out of here without one. It is that serious.'

We have all seen just how important and powerful defibrillators are. The incident at Euro 2020 involving Christian Eriksen showed everyone watching just how vital they are in saving lives. So many people were affected by what they saw on the television that day because footballers are seen by many as being super fit and if a player at the peak of his career can suffer a cardiac arrest, then anyone can. Watching the Danish midfielder collapse on the pitch brought back some uncomfortable memories but the over riding thought for me from the incident is because it happened so publicly in a major tournament that the whole world saw just what a defibrillator can do and hopefully there will now be a concerted effort to have many more throughout all levels of football from the very top to the youngest children just starting to play for their first grassroots teams. They are literally the difference between life and death in such a situation.

The few days after the initial surgery were horrible. I could hardly walk due to the catheters that had been pushed through my groins, and I was in a lot of pain. I then had a few days to wait until my ICD was going to be fitted. Plenty of thinking time and more importantly plenty of time to worry. A few days later, on 25 March, I was taken down to theatre for the second time that week. I was very nervous. I'd had operations throughout my career but this was different. This was my heart.

I'm not someone who shows a lot of emotion and I've got a high pain threshold, but I had felt so bad during the first operation, like I was dying, and it had been a feeling I had never experienced before in my life. Knowing that this was another heart operation where I again had to be awake throughout, I didn't think I could get through it if that same thing happened again. I would rather have been asleep for the surgery but for both operations that week I was wide awake, hearing and seeing everything that was happening.

As I was wheeled down for the operation, we stopped, waiting for the lift. 'You'll Never Walk Alone' was playing loudly from a nearby ward. It's amazing how things like that happen. Almost fate.

From standing on the Kop, singing it with my dad, my brother or my son, to hearing the crowd sing it as a player, to hearing it while lying in a hospital bed before life-changing surgery, it is a song that always means so much to me and this was no different. It gave me the strength to get through another painful operation that Monday afternoon.

Liverpool were brilliant with me, which was nothing short of what I would have expected from such a club. They made sure everything was taken care of in terms of Wendy and me getting to and from London, and Wendy having somewhere to stay for a few days. The academy manager, Alex Inglethorpe, called me on the day of the operation, and has always made it clear both before and after the surgery that the club would be there for me. That was a touch of class from him.

Life was always going to change that day. Having a machine similar to the size of a cigarette box in my chest isn't normal and certainly isn't comfortable. Taking medication in big doses that purposely slows down my heart makes me unbelievably tired and lethargic at times, but both those things give me the opportunity to lead a relatively normal life.

There is no playing football, though; a kickabout with Josh and Olivia is as strenuous as it gets these days. I still go to the gym. I don't do any cardio work, but at least it keeps me active.

Simple things that anyone would take for granted are things I now have to think about and decide whether they are worth the risk. I do feel mentally stronger, however. It's only when you are forced to go through tough times that you realise you are stronger than you think you are.

There will be tougher times to come, I know that. My ICD has to be changed approximately every eight years and the leads that travel through my veins and connect it to my heart have to be replaced every ten years, so there is more heart surgery to come at various stages in my life, and with that comes risk.

As strange as it sounds, I am actually pleased that my defib has shocked me because, as unpleasant as it is, I know I will get through it when it happens again.

That first shock came just a week after my surgery, on 4 April 2019. The shocks hit you hard and aren't things I will ever get used to.

I can still see myself on one knee. My senses slowly coming back to me. My head clearing. Someone was talking to me. I could hear a voice, but I couldn't hear it at the same time. I was there, but I wasn't there.

At first it didn't sink in what had just happened. My ICD had not shocked me up until that point. For a split second it's like you're in a high-speed car crash. Very little warning. Maybe a couple of seconds of dizziness. Then boom.

It's the sound of the defibrillator firing that affects me more than anything else. I'm not even sure if anyone stood next to me would be able to hear the sound of the shock but the noise went right through my body.

As I began to stand up, my first thought was to look behind me as I thought someone had hit me across the back of the head with a baseball bat, before realising what had just happened.

I remember swearing. 'Fuck!' Just one word was all I could manage.

I can still hear myself say it now. The exact tone that I said it in as I started to get up off the floor. There was absolute disbelief in my voice at how powerful the shock had been. Powerful enough to knock me off my feet. The force at which it had hit me was unbelievable, but it had helped to save my life.

I would find out the next day in hospital that my heart had been racing at 241 beats per minute when it kicked in. It soon dawned on me that life had changed in an unimaginable way and would never go back to the normality I'd had before that day.

How do you go from being a fit professional footballer to being afraid to walk down the street for fear of the defibrillator inside your chest shocking you and knocking you over?

After that first 'shock', for the next month the anxiety was beyond anything I had ever experienced. Even walking my daughter Olivia to school scared me to death. Holding her hand on the way was almost for me not her. I couldn't do anything without fear for that month, waiting for the next shock to hit me. I would feel the pacemaker part of my ICD kicking in at the slightest thing as my heart rate rose.

Football helped me massively at that time. Liverpool were going for the Premier League title soI focused on that. I couldn't go to the match, but I was on television duty for a month. My son Josh was at Anfield singing for the two of us. My first game back on the Kop was the second leg of the Champions League semi-final against Barcelona.

'It will be a good one to ease your way back in to going, Dad,' Josh had told me. 'We're not going to score four, are we? Salah is missing and everything.' Four goals later amid delirium in L4, as the unthinkable happened, I knew if I could get through that game and the excitement that went with it without the defib firing then I would be fine.

I didn't need to go, though. Take it easy, relax. It's only football. The words 'only' and 'football' had never managed to fall in the same sentence for me, however.

I probably thought more about my own football career in the months immediately after my heart operation than I had ever done. I had time on my hands, plenty of it. All I did was think. I couldn't relax or sleep properly for weeks. What my life had been like before I knowingly had this condition was all that filled my mind.

I know some people think it is hard for me. I find it harder mentally at times than I do physically, but I don't consider myself unlucky. There are many people far worse off than I am. I have survived a condition that, tragically, kills up to 80 per cent of the people who are affected by it, so I know that I am one of the lucky ones. I'm lucky because I have something inside my chest that will hopefully save my life the next time that I need it to.

And I'm even luckier because my condition didn't hit me until I had finished playing.

So I still got to experience the highs, the lows, the joy, the anguish and the addiction of being a footballer. I could never have lived without any of that.

22

One last game

IF I could play one last game, these are the players I would play alongside from the many team-mates I had during my career. I have listed ten names here, with me completing the 11 as one of two centre-forwards.

GK: PADDY KENNY – BURY

Top goalkeeper and such a normal, likeable, down-to-earth fella off the pitch. At Liverpool I was used to training with David James and Brad Friedel, who were absolute giants. Paddy wasn't like that in stature and was still a young lad learning his trade when I first went to Bury, but he was a fantastic keeper and got better and better as he progressed to the Premier League. As a massive character he was brilliant to have around the dressing room too.

RB: LEE UNSWORTH – BURY

Unsy was my room-mate at Bury and towards the end of one season, when I played wide right, we had a great understanding down that side of the pitch. He could run all day and loved to get forward. I nicked a goal off him against Shrewsbury, but I'm sure I repaid him by making nearly every goal Unsy scored for the club!

LB: MIKE LEA – COLWYN BAY

Leggy had the ability to play in the Football League. At Colwyn Bay, when I played on the left, he would be behind me and we had an influential partnership the season we won promotion. A good defender and a left-back who had great end product when he went forward. A dedicated, hard-working footballer.

CB: JAMIE CARRAGHER – LIVERPOOL

Carra had the most natural enthusiasm of any player I played with. He simply hated losing at anything. He was unbelievably vocal on the pitch. He was a leader and organising those around him was natural to him. He defended as though his life depended on it, gave absolutely everything on the pitch, and his quality on the ball was very underrated.

CB: SIMON GRAND – MORECAMBE

Grandy was captain of the 'Invincibles' at Morecambe and a great lad off the pitch. He had a superb left foot and, despite not being lightning quick, he read the game so well. His goalscoring record for a centre-back in the seasons I played with him was excellent as well. A great talker and leader at the back.

CM: PAUL REID – BURY

I loved Reidy playing behind me at Bury. He had a left foot like a wand. His vision and understanding of the game were brilliant. He was getting on a bit when I joined Bury and I would have loved to have played alongside him in his prime. I'll always be grateful to him for the pass that created my first senior goal, against Peterborough.

RM: CHRIS BILLY – BURY

Ceebs gave you absolutely everything playing on the right. He was another top fella off the pitch and I got on well with him. He scored a few great goals in the years I was with him at Bury.

I don't think he was ever properly appreciated by the fans, but in the dressing room the players knew what he gave us on the pitch.

CM: STEVEN GERRARD – LIVERPOOL

Without doubt the best player I ever played with. A naturally gifted footballer. He had everything. Playing in front of him was brilliant because if you made the right run, he had the ability to play the perfect pass. If you didn't, he would let you know! He would have made any team in the world better had he played for them. He was that good.

CF: COLIN CRAMB – BURY

I played with Cramby at Crewe as well, but never alongside him up front. When he came to Bury we just hit it off instantly as a strike partnership. He would come short to get on the ball while I would make the runs in behind, and we caused teams so many problems by making goals for each other. He was the life and soul of any dressing room and we got on brilliantly off the pitch as well.

LM: CARL BAKER – MORECAMBE

Bakes had unbelievable natural ability and loved having the ball at his feet. He could score and make goals and rose from non-league football to playing in the Championship. At times he looked like he had the ball on a string as he went on mazy runs, taking on defenders, and always looked like he could make things happen.

MANAGER

I worked with some great managers. Gérard Houllier gave me my Liverpool debut, which I will never forget. Dave Challinor at Colwyn Bay did an incredible job and was so organised; his attention to detail was second to none and he has everything needed to manage at a high level. But Andy Preece at Bury knew how to get the best out of me and gave me the belief that I needed.I spent the happiest and best two years of my career playing under him at Gigg Lane.

23

Coming full circle

AFTER I finished playing for Walshaw, I was fortunate enough to join up with Dave Challinor and Colin Woodthorpe again when Chall asked me to work with AFC Fylde's under-18s every morning. I was soon working more and more with the first-team as one of the coaches and it was five months that I enjoyed immensely as the club tried to gain promotion from National League North into the top tier of non-league football.

The club had everything that was needed to gain promotion. The infrastructure was all there with a stadium that would not have looked out of place in League 1 or 2, as were the resources to pay significant transfer fees for players and most importantly they had the quality of players to win the league.

It was fantastic to have that day-to-day involvement in full-time first-team football again and I really enjoyed working with the players as Chall and Col successfully brought the title to Mill Farm. I felt very much part of the club thanks to those two and the players.

I would have loved to have continued in that role, but I was also working part time at Liverpool's academy and had been for more than two years. So I would be working at Fylde during the day and then going straight to the academy in Kirkby for evening training. Have boots, will travel!

The academy manager, Alex Inglethorpe, offered me a full-time coaching role at Liverpool working with the under-11s and the opportunity, with some top coaches and people, was too good to turn down.

On returning to the club, I coached for two years alongside my good mate Carl Lancaster, and with the brilliantly inventive coach Michael Beale overseeing the younger age groups at that time it was such an enjoyable couple of years where I learnt so much.

It was as though I was coming full circle back to the club where I had started as a nine-year-old, but this time it would be me trying to guide the youngsters as Steve Heighway, Hugh McAuley and Dave Shannon had guided me.

I had been so fortunate to learn from the best and it would be my job to help to play a very small part in trying to produce more players to follow in their dreams of walking out in front of the Kop in that famous red shirt.

Since the heart surgery my role at the club has changed. I'm no longer coaching but I'm still working full time at Liverpool, now in academy player recruitment, which I enjoy. It is yet another very different side to the game that I get to experience.

The addiction I have to football is still as strong as ever. It always will be. That will never change. Football will always be one of the most important things in my life.

My journey, from Anfield to almost everywhere has certainly been eventful.

Acknowledgements

Martin Ogden – Former club photographer at Bury FC – cover photo
David Bell @tontastic – Twitter
Martin Lyons – Colwyn Bay FC photo

Thank you to all the team at Pitch Publishing for believing in the book.

Thanks to Hugh McAuley for writing the foreword for this book. H wasn't only my football coach for all those years, he was and still is a mentor and a great friend of mine.

Thank you to both my brother David and journalist Tim Channon for their advice in the preparation of this book.

Thank you to Alex Inglethorpe, Liverpool Football Club and all my colleagues at Liverpool FC Academy for the support they showed me during the diagnosis and aftermath of my heart condition. I will be forever grateful.

Also available at all good book stores

9781785316470

9781785313929

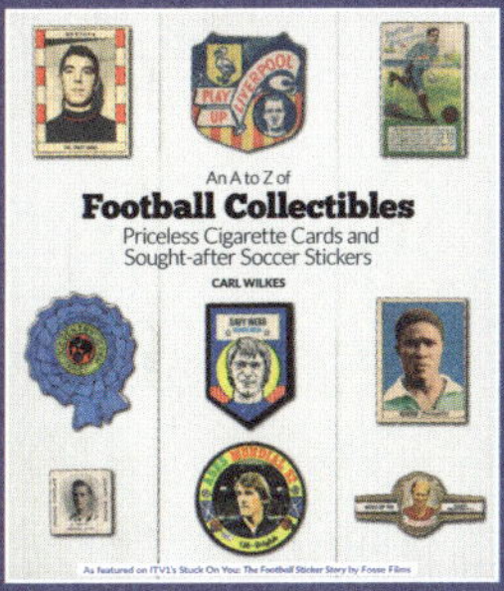

9781785315602

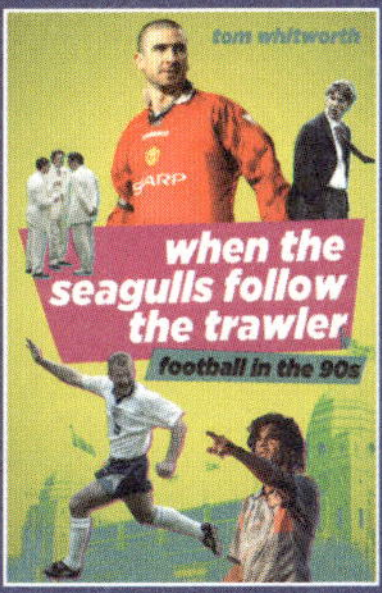

9781785317613

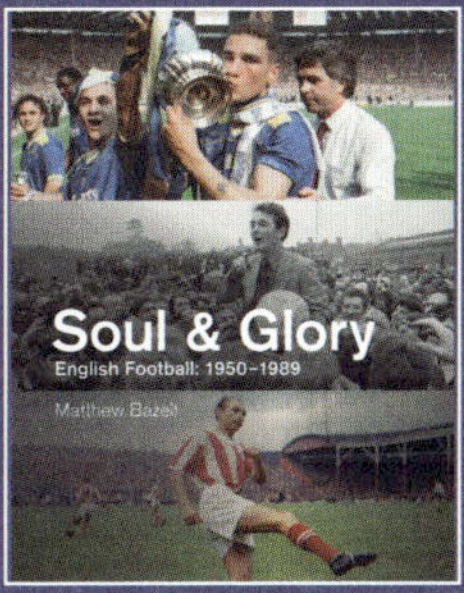

9781801500067

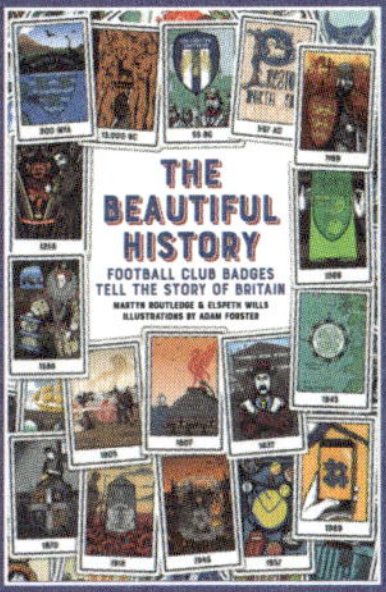

9781785317927

9781785319914

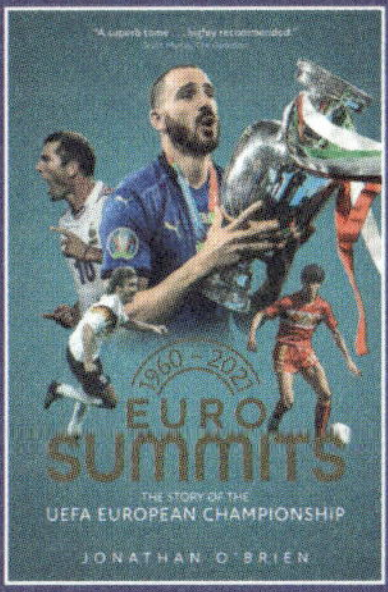

9781801501125

9781801500005